SNOW O
THE EQU

H. W. TILMAN

Mount Kenya: Joseph Glacier and Point Piggott,
showing col at foot of the west ridge

SNOW ON THE EQUATOR

H. W. TILMAN

TILMAN
www.tilmanbooks.com

First published 1937 by G. Bell and Sons Ltd
This edition published 2015 by Tilman Books,
a joint venture by
Lodestar Books www.lodestarbooks.com
and Vertebrate Publishing www.v-publishing.com

Original text copyright © Simon Heyworth Davis 1937
Foreword copyright © Sir Chris Bonington 2015

Cover design by Jane Beagley
Vertebrate Graphics Ltd. www.v-graphics.co.uk

Lodestar Books has asserted its right
to be identified as the Editor of this Work

Series editor Dick Wynne
Series researcher Bob Comlay

The publisher has made reasonable effort to locate
the holders of copyright in the illustrations in this book,
and will be pleased to hear from them regarding
correct attribution in future editions

A CIP catalogue record for this book
is available from the British Library

ISBN 978-1-909461-14-7

Typeset in Baskerville from Storm Type Foundry
Printed and bound by Pulsio, Bulgaria
All papers used by Tilman Books are sourced responsibly

Contents

Photographs

Maps

The pen and ink drawings in the text were tailpieces to some chapters in the first edition, and are by 'Bip' Pares (Ethel Pares, 1904–1977), a prominent and prolific book illustrator, cover designer and poster artist of the 1920s–1950s. She and her second husband Robert Bradby spent their honeymoon in the Himalaya, travelling with H. W. Tilman's 1938 Everest expedition.

Note that Chapters V and VI have the same title—this is not an error.

Foreword

Sir Chris Bonington

In Jim Perrin's excellent introduction to the collected works of Tilman's mountain writing, he describes the man as 'unsurpassed as a mountaineering author'. I would like to say that Jim hasn't quite gone far enough in his praise, for in looking closely at Tilman and his lifetime exploring the world's mountains, one has to think long and hard to find someone who surpasses his record, not only as an author, but also as a mountaineer. I urge all young adventurers to read a little of Tilman before setting off on their own endeavours, as we did, if only to keep one's self-importance and ego firmly buried in the bottom of the rucksack. His boldness, organisation, and sheer sense of adventure make him one of the greatest mountaineers and explorers Britain has ever known. His list of first ascents around the world, many of which he tackled simply to see what lay beyond the summit, are still not fully appreciated. It is therefore a great pleasure, and not before time, that we see his fifteen wonderfully written books now being republished as new editions.

Climbers of my generation often went to remote mountains, we often tried new routes—we saw ourselves as pioneers, but more often we were shadows, following in the footsteps of Tilman and his friends. I have always found it an inspiration to read his books and share some of his enthusiasm for the unexplored world.

Snow on the Equator introduces us to the young Bill Tilman who, in his own words, was looking for something to do:

> *To those who went to the War straight from school and survived it,*
> *the problem of what to do afterwards was peculiarly difficult.*

Snow on the Equator, Tilman's first book, shows the young man, looking for adventure but also searching to understand his own personality. He had left Britain, left the memories it held of time spent in the trenches during the War, and gone out to find a new life in Africa. He met up with Eric Shipton and together they formed one of the most iconic climbing partnerships in British history. It was in Africa that Tilman succeeded in a series of endeavours, including ascents of Kilimanjaro, a traverse of Mount Kenya and a 3000-mile bike ride home. All are recounted with great humour, and between the lines we discover more of the man who would go on to see so much of the last unexplored corners of the globe.

CB
May 2015

CHAPTER I

TEN YEARS' HARD

Young soldier, what will you be,
When it's all over?
I shall get out and across the sea,
Where land's cheap and a man can thrive.

—MAX PLOWMAN

TO THOSE WHO WENT TO THE WAR straight from school and survived it, the problem of what to do afterwards was peculiarly difficult. A loss of three or four years upset preconceived plans, and while the War was in progress little thought was devoted to such questions. Not that there was no opportunity for thinking, for there was ample time for that during solitary night watches at observation post or gun line; during periods of what was euphemistically called 'resting' behind the lines; or, where most of us went sooner or later, in hospital. No, the reason was because making plans seemed rather a waste of time. Either the War would go on interminably, in which case one was already arranged for, or, in the other alternative, consolation might be found in the philosophy of Feeble, that 'he who dies this year is quit for the next.'

Coming home, then, from the Rhine in April 1919, with what the polite friend might call an 'open' and the candid a blank mind, it was not altogether surprising that in August of the same year I found myself on a cargo-boat bound for East Africa, or B.E.A. as it was then called. My destination was simply accounted for by the fact that I had drawn a farm, or rather a square mile of land, in a lottery for ex-Service men; and the conveyance, because that seemed to be the quickest way of getting there. And since our destination was believed to be a place where, speaking metaphorically, pearls could be picked up on the beach, it was impossible for one to be on the spot too soon.

When the War had ended there were so many Colonials and others awaiting repatriation, or anxious to begin new jobs abroad, that passages were at a premium. The shipping offices were besieged, and had waiting-lists miles long. One was told dark stories, which I am sure were libellous, of the necessity of bribing the clerks if one's name was to appear in the first few thousands. To avoid this indefinite delay, seven of this impatient horde, including myself, were impetuous enough to pay thirty-five pounds for the privilege of a passage to Mombasa on the S.S. —.

Five of us were quartered in a steel deckhouse on the poop, flanked on either side by a pen of live sheep, and immediately below was the lascar crew's galley, whence the fumes of cooking never ceased rising. At all seasons of the year the striking thing about the Red Sea, and one that is taken for granted, is the heat, but in August, and in a steel deckhouse with no fans, even Shadrach, Meshach, and Abednego might have remarked on it.

British East Africa—Kenya as it now is—occupies a central position on the east coast of Africa astride the equator. It has undergone many changes since starting life as a chartered company, becoming first a Protectorate and then a Colony, and as such assuming the name it now bears. Its neighbours, too, have changed. It marches on the south what was formerly German East Africa and is now British Mandated Territory of Tanganyika, while on the north it is now bounded by Italian territory instead of Abyssinian. West is Uganda, which still stands where it did, and on the east is the sea, one of the few unchanging things left in a changing world.

In the closing years of last century British interests in East Africa, represented mainly by missionaries and the Chartered Company of British East Africa, were centred in Uganda. In 1893 the Imperial Government took over from the company, and the favourable reports of administrators like Lugard and Portal, the pressure of missionary influence at home, and fear of French designs in the Sudan, combined to bring about the construction of the Uganda railway from Mombasa on the coast to Kisumu on the eastern shore of Lake Victoria. An East African Protectorate was declared in 1902, and the healthy, fertile uplands lying beyond the arid coastal belt, which the railway had now reached, began to attract the attention of a few enterprising pioneers. The higher and better parts were uninhabited except for the nomadic Masai, who so dominated the country that the other tribes,

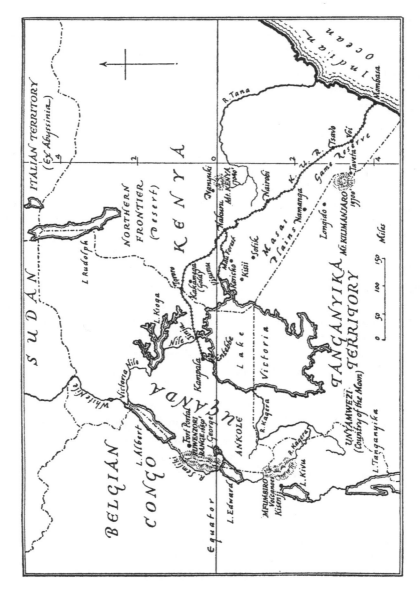

Map 1: Lake Victoria and surrounding territories

for peace's sake, confined themselves to the forest and bush. Grants of land in the Highlands, as they were called, were made to individuals and companies (a small matter of five hundred square miles to one of the last), and there was some talk of making the Highlands a Jewish National Home—Palestine not being available at that time. By 1914 there were a few hundred settlers, mostly engaged in cattle farming and coffee growing, and Nairobi was already a place of some importance as the capital of the Protectorate.

Prior to the War, Nairobi had some notoriety on account of occasional ebullitions of high feeling on the part of the settlers against the too fatherly attitude of the Government. After the War it was notorious for another reason. Lurid stories were told of the guile and rapacity of those who lay in wait in the Nairobi bars to separate the new settler from his capital, so that the innocent and fearful, like myself, hardly dared to have a drink, kept both hands in their pockets, and passed through the town as quickly as possible. So it came about that in October (the voyage having lasted for six weeks) I was viewing from the top of a tree the square mile of land which was to be my home for the next ten years. This unusual method of inspection was adopted because heavy bush, through which there were no paths, for there were no inhabitants, prevented access to it; and from a tree on a neighbouring ridge a much better notion of its features and possibilities could be got than by submerging oneself in a sea of bush and fighting a way across.

I knew nothing about land, and less about farming it, but the climate of this district was said to be good both from a coffee-growing and a health standpoint. I could see for myself that the land was watered by several streams and one large river, while the growth of forest and bush on it clearly indicated that the soil was good. True, it was in the back blocks fifty miles from the railway, a journey of three or four days for ox-wagons, which were then the only means of transport; no Europeans had grown anything there before, and the clearing of the land would be an expensive business; but all that weighed light in the balance against the ardour of the pioneer, the thought of owning land (and such a large chunk), and, to quote Dr Johnson, 'the potentiality of growing rich beyond the dreams of avarice.' When added to this was the knowledge that the financial conditions attached to the acceptance of it were easy, it will be understood that I was not long in making up my mind.

Another settler who had arrived here in August was in occupation of some land about one and a half miles from where I proposed to make my home. B. was a newcomer to the district and to farming, but not to B.E.A., since he had worked in Nairobi for a short time before the War. He had then served in the Northern Frontier District near the Abyssinian border with the King's African Rifles before being moved to France, so that he knew enough of the language, the conditions, and the natives, to make the month I now spent with him of great value to me. We lived together in a tent, and began a friendship that ended only with his tragic death seven years later.

The land was situated on the south-western slopes of the Mau Forest, between the edge of the forest and a native reserve, at an elevation of 6500 feet. Though within less than a degree of the equator, the shade temperature seldom exceeded eighty degrees and at night dropped to fifty degrees or lower. It was a country of narrow ridges and spurs, of steep valleys, covered with bush, bracken, and scattered forest. There was little or no grass, and near the streams the forest grew thickly. The earth was a deep red loam, remarkable for its uniformity and the absence of stone, sand, or clay, the lack of which was a severe handicap when it came to putting up buildings that were expected to last more than a year or two.

From the station an earth cart-road ran south for twenty-one miles to Kericho, the administrative post for the Lumbwa Reserve, whence it continued for another fifty miles to the Sotik District before fading out into the blue. This road passed within four miles of our land, but in between ran a river, thirty to forty feet wide, too swift and deep to ford except in the 'dry weather' period from November to March.

Obviously the first thing to be done was to bridge this river and make a road of access to the main road, so this was the task that absorbed most of our energies during the month I spent with B. The river was then low, and it behoved us to get the job finished before the rains began in March. Its proximity to the Mau Forest on the one hand, and the fact that the great water mass of Lake Victoria was only forty miles away on the other, made the district a wet one. The average rainfall was over sixty inches a year, and was so well distributed that

January was the only month when a long spell of dry weather could be counted upon.

We built a fearsome structure of four spans of twelve feet, carried on clumsy but solid wooden piers. Single logs were tied together with iron dog-spikes, and the whole pier coiled round with barbed wire in much the same way as the drunken 'Brugglesmith'* bound himself to his stretcher as he gyrated down the street pulling the bell-wire after him. Barbed wire is more conveniently used for fencing than for lashing bridge piers. Large quantities had been used recently for the long and elaborate fences stretching from Switzerland to the sea, but, the demand for wire for this purpose having fortunately ceased, miles of it could now be bought for an old song, and that, of course, was our sole reason for using it. We found it just as intractable and spiteful to handle here as it had been in France.

The steep river-banks were heavily wooded, so that timber for the bridge was plentiful, but we had to rely entirely upon the natives for expert knowledge about the suitability of different types of tree. Much bitter experience was needed before we acquired this very necessary knowledge ourselves, and, meanwhile, for any building operations of ours, the natives naturally selected trees with an eye to their proximity, or the ease with which they could be felled, rather than for their powers of resistance to water or white ants. So that this first bridge of ours lasted only for a year, and most of our earlier huts and sheds were devoured standing by the all-pervading termite. Until we built a steel and concrete bridge over a similar river bounding the property on the other side, communications were always liable to interruption. The fate of every cart that left, or was due to return, was a source of anxious speculation until we knew whether it was across the bridge or in the river, while during every spell of wet weather and the accompanying spate in the river it was the usual thing to walk down to the bridge of an evening to see if it was still there.

Feeling a slightly less vivid shade of green after my month with B., I returned to Nairobi, and a week later started again for what I now liked to call my estate, taking with me an assortment of carts, ploughs, harrows, tools, household gear, and food. Having hired some oxen

---

*   A character in Kipling—*Ed.*

and their drivers at the station, the two light carts (army transport carts ex-German East) were loaded up, the oxen inspanned, and B.'s place reached four days later. The bridge was not quite finished, but it was solid enough for B. to cut the silk ribbon, as it were, and declare the bridge open. The carts crossed in triumph at the run, with the oxen, encouraged by fierce cries and whip-flourishing from the drivers, leaning hard against each other and away from the rushing water.

Word was now passed round by B.'s boys that another white man wanted labour, and soon I had a small gang at work clearing a track through the mile and a half of bush to my future home. I took up my residence in a tent on the highest land of all, and started the gang, which had now increased to fifty, cutting the bush on a long, gently sloping hillside where I proposed turning the first furrow. Other boys began training oxen to make up the necessary teams, and this was a process which forcibly suggested to the inexperienced onlooker a bloodless bull-fight. Unless one was both callous and nimble it was advisable to be busy elsewhere while this was in progress. A good deal of beating and tail-twisting was necessary to produce results, for an ox has a very effective trick of lying down and remaining down when asked to do anything unusual. Before things got to that stage, even before the animal had been captured and yoked, there would be many fierce rushes which put the fear of death into the clothed, booted, and clumsy white man, but only amused the naked and agile Lumbwa.

Meantime, accompanied by one or two boys armed with 'pangas,' or machetes, to clear a way, I began to find out how my land lay, and soon discovered that there were more eligible sites for a house than where the tent was now pitched. A sheltered position, room for a garden, a view, and water near at hand, were the essentials, and there was more than one place where all these could be had. As I grudged spending time or money on a house while the more important work of development remained to be done, the house was to be only a mud and wattle affair, so that no great harm would be done if it turned out to be in the wrong place. Two, in fact, were built in different places before I was satisfied I had found the best, and before I began to build, many years later, something more substantial.

The first had all the stern virtue of simplicity—a single square room without doors or windows. That is to say, there were two apertures, a larger one for the door and a smaller one for the window, but nothing that needed opening or shutting. A small veranda was cunningly built on in front, where in the daytime I fed, because the living-room was too dark. It was fitted with a chair and table by the simple expedient of driving into the ground four stakes which supported small straight sticks. The floor was of earth, of which one advantage was that you could light a fire on it, or, when I had reached a more advanced stage of civilisation and could spare the tin, a brazier. Close as we were to the equator, the altitude made the nights cool enough for a fire to be welcome all the year round.

There were, however, one or two drawbacks to an earth floor. Bracken and creepers grew up through it as if they were being 'forced,' and had to be cut down frequently; it became dry and dusty, so that the boy sweeping it with an improvised bracken broom lowered it by several inches a month. (It was not wise to tell him to be less vigorous, or the floor might not have been swept at all.) Moreover, it held a great attraction for the hens, who liked coming in to scratch holes in which they could enjoy a dust bath and lay eggs. Encouraged by these ideal conditions, the jigger flea made its appearance. This is a very small insect which burrows under toe-nails and finger-nails, where it is only discovered by the intense irritation it sets up. It has then to be extracted by digging round it with a needle, an operation which is only complete when the whole insect, with its newly formed egg-sac, has been removed. Houseboys, hens, and dogs are the main sources of flea-infection, but in this district the jigger did not seem to find conditions very congenial. A liberal sprinkling of the earth floor with some disinfectant like Jeyes' (which the boys called 'cheese'), or even water, kept them in check, while with a wood floor they were practically unknown. The jigger, or chegoe, is indigenous to South America, and is supposed to have been brought over to the west coast of Africa in the sand ballast of a ship early in the last century. From there, within a short time, it spread across Africa to the east coast.

Of the plagues and pests usually associated with the tropics we were singularly free; at least, of those which annoy man; but with crops and livestock it was quite another matter. Mosquitoes were rare, while those few we had were not infected with malaria. It was too cold for scorpions. Hornets and snakes were only occasional visitors. I remember killing a puff adder in the garden, and nearly being killed by a bright green snake sitting in a coffee-bush which I had just started to prune; and many years later, after the petrol age had dawned, I found a puff adder enjoying the lingering warmth on the cylinder head of a car when I opened the bonnet in the morning. But the number seen or killed on the farm annually could be counted on one hand, and, though the natives were mortally afraid of snakes, even dead ones, I never heard of anyone, European or native, being bitten.

The white ant was always with us, but it, fortunately, is not carnivorous, and feeds exclusively on any wood stuck in the ground or in contact with the ground. It never comes to the surface, so that the posts, the rafters, and even the thatch of a house, can be honeycombed with ants without any visible sign of their activities except a few bits of earth, like wormcasts, on the outside of the wood. Certain woods— cedar, for instance—they will not touch, but most posts have to be sunk in concrete. Nor is the wood of a roof or ceiling resting on a brick wall safe, for the ants find a way up to it through the wall between the bricks. The worker termites, which do all the damage, are white, and cannot stand the light of day, hence the earth which they stick on the outside of a post to keep their runs dark.

More ferocious are the black soldier or safari ants, and the red, tree ants, which attack anything living that comes in their way, but an occasional visit from safari ants is not without benefit to a grass hut, to which they give a very thorough spring cleaning. The roof of a grass hut and the mud walls harbour an astonishing variety of insects, of which the least revolting are the spiders and the most obscene a great, fat, white slug. None of these obtrude on one if left alone, and the only indications of their presence are mysterious rustling noises at night, a slight but constant shower of sawdust sent down by the borer beetles, bits of grass dislodged by some restless slug, and occasionally the arrival of some kind of insect in person on the bed or in the soup. But that unpleasantness can be avoided by using a ceiling-cloth or sleeping under a mosquito net, while the safari ants can be relied upon to clear the whole lot out periodically.

If their visit takes place in the daytime, little inconvenience is caused, for one simply vacates the house and waits until they have cleaned up the livestock. The houseboy may make futile attempts to deflect their line of march with barriers of hot embers, but if the army is in strength this is a useless expedient. A few hours after taking possession they will have devoured every live and dead insect in the hut and passed on their way.

At night it is a different matter. The first indication of trouble is an intensification of the rustling sounds in the roof, but this warning may go unheeded and, presently, if not under a net, one is awakened by a sharp stab in the arm or some more sensitive spot, or by one of the fat slugs, smothered with ants, dropping from the roof on to one's face. You must then 'stand not upon the order of your going,' but make a dive for the door, picking up several hundred ants off the floor *en route*, and, when well clear of the marauding host and its far-flung scouts, tear off your pyjamas and proceed to pull off the numerous ants which have now got their fangs well buried in all the most inaccessible parts of your body. If you have had time to rescue some blankets and a camp-bed, all is well, for on several occasions I have been thus driven out and spent the rest of the night bedded down in a store or tool-shed.

Bats were another source of disturbed nights. Three or four might find their way into the room at the same time, where they seemed to delight in brushing past one's face as close as possible. The thought of being touched by their clammy wings and mouse-like, flea-ridden bodies was revolting, and I found it impossible to sleep so long as one remained fluttering about. I used to light the lamp and be in bed holding a .22 rifle, to pot them off one by one whenever they settled and hung head downwards from a beam, as sooner or later they did. A quicker and more sporting method was to bag them flying with a tennis racquet.

While on the subject of pests, one of a more serious, widespread, and devastating kind, amounting, in fact, to a plague, should not escape notice. This was the invasion of Kenya and neighbouring East African territories by the desert locust, which began in 1928 and continued for three or four years. The southern deserts of the distant Sudan were their source of origin, but once a swarm is allowed to lay eggs and hatch out it multiplies itself in a way which defies arithmetic. So serious was the destruction of food crops, both native and European, that at one period the export of foodstuffs was forbidden for fear of famine. It was no uncommon thing to see a swarm take a whole day to pass overhead, veiling the sun as it went, or for a swarm to settle and strip two or three hundred acres of maize or wheat in a very short time. Coffee was about the only green stuff they appeared not to eat, but they did almost as much damage by settling on it and breaking the branches with their weight. There were stories of their eating even the thatch of a roof; one man, it was said, having his roof eaten over his head while he was in his bath. But perhaps such stories were apocryphal.

My second dwelling was a more elaborate affair, built on another site, and finished not a moment too soon, for the old hut collapsed the day I moved into the new one. This house was another wattle and daub structure, but it consisted of two big six-sided huts connected by a veranda, open to the front. It had a fireplace of sun-dried bricks, and a wood floor made from planks cut by the small circular saw which was now in use at B.'s place. (B., who had worked at a saw-mill, got a lot of fun out of slicing up big logs. His main trouble was to prevent boys putting their hands on it to see if it was going round.) From the house I could command a view of the whole planted area of the farm, but, in spite of this encouragement to do so, I did not adopt the practice of 'farming from the veranda,' a common East African failing. Across the valley of the Itare River one looked over the green, broken, but uninteresting country of the Lumbwa Reserve, and beyond to the low wall of the Kisii Hills bounding the western horizon, hills which were washed to a deep indigo after the storms which broke on them had passed away.

The reason for the dullness of the view across the Reserve was, I think, a complete absence of trees; a common feature, sooner or later, of all native Reserves. It is brought about by their system of cultivation and their goats. Each family will clear an acre, or half an acre, of new land every season for their crop of maize or wimbi (a small millet), while the innumerable goats see to it that no seedling trees survive to replace those thus annually destroyed. In the more populated parts of the Reserve it was a source of wonder as to where the natives collected enough sticks for fuel, and for the light fencing which they put round the fields to keep out the ubiquitous goat. As these goats produce neither milk nor hair, and as they are used for food only on the occasion of certain festivals, they are in themselves almost valueless. Their chief function is to figure as a form of currency in such transactions as the purchase of wives or cattle, in the payment of fines, or in the feeing of the witch-doctor. The destruction of the trees, of course, encourages 'wash,' denudes the soil of humus, and may even affect the rainfall. The evil is obvious, and, though something is being done to repair the damage by encouraging tree-planting, the root of the evil is difficult to remove without considerably altering the native's mode of living.

The most attractive part of the view, at any rate to me, was, in course of time, the neat parallel rows of alternating coffee-bushes and shade-trees stretching away from below the house for half a mile. Most pleasing of all was it when in blossom, with the white flowers set off against the rich dark green of the leaves, or, six months later, when promise had come to fruition, and the bright red cherry-like berries weighed down the branches. It sounds magnificent and it looked magnificent, but in later years it became an increasingly infrequent sight. Hail might knock off all the flower, or even prevent the trees flowering; the flowers when formed acquired an unfortunate habit of not 'setting'; and, if the fruit did appear, it presently acquired a nasty way of turning black and dropping off long before it had reached the cherry-ripe stage. In the six, seven, or even eight months between flower and harvest there was so much that might happen, and so much that did.

During our first few years most of our energy and capital were devoted to the growing of flax. This commodity was fetching a very high price at the end of the War, and for the first year or two after it. Our mouths watered when we heard of one lot of Kenya flax which sold for £400 a ton, and calculations of profit based on a price of £200 a ton seemed fair, and were undoubtedly attractive. When estimating profits, it should be a safe rule to halve the probable returns and double the estimated expenses, but we were to find that even then two and two sometimes made three.

Eager to take advantage of the high price, we worked feverishly to clear, stump, plough, and sow as many acres as possible. My first year I got in fifty acres, while in succeeding years the acreage sown to flax, if not always reaped, was near a hundred. The snag about flax-growing is that, though the growing of it is fairly simple, the harvesting is not the end of one's troubles, but only the beginning. The ripe stalks have all to be pulled up by the roots by hand, dried on the field in stooks, and stored in a barn. When the weather is favourable—that is, not too much sun and not too much rain—it is taken out and spread thinly and evenly, almost stalk by stalk, on grass, to undergo what is called 'dew-retting.' This process takes ten to fourteen days, according to the weather, during which time it has to be turned frequently. If there is too much rain it goes mouldy, while too much sun weakens the fibre. After that it is stooked again, tied in bundles, and once more stored in a barn until it can be scutched. With ten or fifteen acres of ground covered with retted flax, ready to carry, the awaiting of the necessary dry day in the middle of a wet spell was a most wearing business for the poor farmer, when every day longer that it remained out meant a serious deterioration in quality and loss in value.

For the scutching, machinery is needed, and it was nearly three years after I started that the first flax was scutched at B.'s and shipped home to England. During this time we had watched the market for flax drop first to £200 and then to £100, at which figure my first lot was sold. Then the rot set in, and before another year was out we were receiving only £50 a ton, a lower price than we had previously obtained for our tow, a by-product of the scutching process. A few farmers in Kenya were ruined by flax, and most lost money by it; especially those who, like my neighbours B. and his partner, had put money into flax machinery. I was fortunate myself, but unless the machinery had been put up it would not have been any use growing flax.

However, even from the beginning, neither my neighbours nor myself had banked entirely on flax, because there were several factors besides the fickleness of the market and the vagaries of the weather which made it an uneconomic crop for us. The yield was low (about half that which is obtained in Europe), a tropical sun weakened the fibre and made it a poorer quality, and we found that it was impossible to crop the same land more than twice. This meant that, to maintain the acreage, fresh land had to be cleared and broken every year, adding greatly to the cost of production; and, apart from that, it was an immoral proceeding in that it partook more of mining the land than farming it, taking good out of it and putting nothing back—exactly what our friends the natives were doing in their Reserve on the other side of the river.

Coffee was the alternative crop, and, after the first year, twenty or thirty acres were planted annually, so that, when flax was finally dropped, five years later, there was a substantial acreage of coffee, the oldest of which was just coming into bearing. Entitled now to call myself a planter, which sounds so much more dashing than farmer, I felt that a mud and grass hut was hardly worthy of my new status. The planter's bungalow of the novelist is generally spacious, if not luxurious. Even the assistant manager's bungalow is 'trim,' and, in both, servants in spotless white hover silently at their master's elbow. Only planters who have lost their job through drink or women, and have very nearly 'gone native,' are allowed to live in grass huts, and to have their gin poured out by a boy attired in a blanket.

So I began my third and last house. It was built of burnt bricks made on the spot, roofed with corrugated iron, and possessed the usual amenities—a floor, a ceiling, doors, glass windows, cupboards, and, not least, a fireplace and a brick chimney. When it was completed with living-room, two bedrooms, veranda, and built-in kitchen, so astonished and impressed were the houseboy and the cook that they demanded a rise in wages and a uniform.

The method of construction was original. I put the roof up first on poles, and then, when the walls were built, taking the poles away, I lowered the roof on to the wall-plate. The reason for this was that the bricks of the inside walls were only sun-dried and not burnt, and so the walls had to be protected from rain as they were built, while in the first place the roof had to serve as a covering for the kiln in which the bricks were burnt. The new house, and therefore the brick-kiln, was sited immediately behind the old one; so close that I had to sit up throughout one night to see that the red-hot wall of the kiln did not set fire to the grass roof of the old house in which I was still living.

Had it caught fire, I might have said with some truth that the new house rose phoenix-like from the ashes of the old. Nevertheless, something of the sort did take place, because when all was ready the old house was abolished almost as rapidly as the felling of a chimney, and there the neat, but not too spacious, bungalow of the novelist stood revealed in all its glory.

The house and my faith in its solidity were severely tested shortly after I had moved in. The whole Colony was put into a state of alarm by a severe earth tremor—a mild earthquake, in fact—which at one place opened cracks in the earth and brought down buildings. The effect was

The first dwelling.

The second.

Third, and last.

Dwellings

less violent in our district, but sufficiently frightening. It happened in
the early hours of the morning, when I was awakened by a sort of roar,
rather like that of an approaching train. At this ominous prelude dogs
barked, cocks crowed, cattle lowed, and then the bed began to shake
violently. For what seemed like a minute, but what was probably only
a few seconds, I lay in bed wondering what would happen next. Then
there was a loud crash, and I streaked for the open spaces, while the
roar receded in the distance. That was the finish of it, and after a decent
interval of time, when confidence was restored, I returned to the house
to find an inch crack opened in the upper half of the wall over my bed,
and a big rhino horn, whose proper place was on the wall, now on the
floor. The fall of that had made the crash which lent wings to my flight.

At the end of one year in my new house, and ten on the farm, I sold
out. Many were the changes that had taken place in that time. New settlers had come, old ones had gone. In a small community such as ours,
births, marriages, and deaths become almost family affairs. Communications had improved greatly, particularly with the station, the negotiation of which road had interested us perhaps more than anything
else. The motor-car and the lorry were now the normal form or transport, and the ox-wagon almost an anachronism. The road had been
widened, re-graded, drained, but it was still unmetalled, so that a prolonged wet spell soon gave rise to quagmires from which, if entered,
it was impossible to escape. Chains for the wheels were a *sine qua non*
on any journey, no matter how fine the weather appeared, while in wet
weather shovels, pangas, planks, old sacks, rabbit-netting, or even a
block and tackle, were all items of equipment that would be carried by
the prudent driver. I remember on one occasion, through neglect of
some such precaution, having to put my waterproof under a spinning
back wheel for want of anything handy to make it grip. That was the
last service it rendered.

For those ten years, except for an annual shooting excursion and
one brief visit to England, I had kept my nose to the grindstone. I saw
no one else except at weekends, so that, in spite of the efforts of kind
neighbours, there was some danger of my becoming as mossy and as
difficult to uproot as some of the bigger trees which had taken us days
to stump; of developing into the sort of person who in another planting
community is called a 'hill-topper'; a man who has lived by himself for

so long that he dreads meeting anyone, and therefore builds his house on the top of some hill, so as to have timely warning of the approach of visitors to escape into the safety of the neighbouring bush.

Another impelling motive for change of scene was that the daily routine of attending to planted coffee was much less congenial to me than the earlier struggle to carve a home out of the forest and to tame the wilderness; to watch the landscape—a waste of bush and jungle, but a familiar one—change daily under one's eyes; to see a new clearing here, a shed there, paths and roads pushing out in all directions, while seeds, which one had oneself planted, grew into trees big enough to make timber.

I already had some land in the Sotik, thirty miles further from the railway, where this absorbing task could be tackled afresh; where with a newly acquired partner there would be no danger of becoming enslaved by the farm. If either wanted a holiday, it could be taken; all that was needed between the two of us was the sort of understanding that John Jorrocks had with his huntsman, James Pigg, to wit, 'that master and man should not both get drunk on the same day.'

CHAPTER II

BUFFALOES—AND FALSE TEETH

For now I am in a holiday humour.

—SHAKESPEARE

IT HAS BEEN HINTED THAT during this first ten years the treadmill on occasion ceased to revolve, and a number of brief excursions were made. By way of comparison, it will be interesting to recall some of these before going on to tell of the more distant tours which I was able to make as a result of the excellent arrangement come to between my partner and myself, as narrated at the end of the last chapter.

Possibly the most urgent desire of the newcomer to a country of big game is to go out and kill something. Fortunately for most, this unsporting blood-lust is soon satiated. The pursuit may be abandoned altogether, or reserved solely for dangerous game, which is a less one-sided affair, or perhaps forsaken for hunting with the camera. One of the many compensations for living in East Africa, if any are needed, is the facility for indulging these desires. I refer particularly to the low cost, for if, on these trips of three or four weeks which we made, we spent over and above the cost of a shooting licence (£10), we thought it an expensive holiday. At the other end of the scale is the visitor, whose licence costs him £100, who may spend up to £100 a month while out on safari, and who, having collected a number of trophies, will be faced by a thumping bill for the mounting of them.

As a newcomer to B.E.A. I was no exception. I was bent on slaughter, and read with avidity every book on hunting that I could lay my hands on; Neumann, Selous, Stigand, and Bell were my mentors. Neumann, who from his skill with the rifle was called by his boys 'Risasi moja' (one cartridge) or 'Nyama jango' (my meat); Selous, who was not only a mighty hunter, but naturalist, pioneer, and soldier, meeting a soldier's death in German East when he was over sixty; Stigand, soldier, too, and administrator, who was always careful to insist on the difference between 'hunting' and 'shooting'—the one in which wits, skill, and endurance are needed to track down and bring to bag the quarry in thick bush or forest, while for the other, which can only be done on the open plains, skill with the rifle is the sole requisite. And lastly Bell—'Karamoja Bell,' Karamoja being the name of his stamping-ground in Eastern Uganda—who used to kill his elephants with a .266 rifle, a very small bore, at times standing on something resembling a surveyor's plane-table to enable him to see over the long grass into which he had followed them.

On the farm there was no outlet for this pent-up desire, for there was little game except wild pig and bush buck, while the growth was too dense to allow any chance of shooting these. I think, in all the years spent there, the total bag was a leopard, a serval cat, and a wild pig. The leopard was tracked down, surrounded, and despatched (when he broke) by several hundred natives armed with spear and shield, at the cost of a badly torn scalp. B. and I were present, armed to the teeth, but were not called upon to do anything bold except to put back the scalp and sew it up. Our antiseptic methods were not thought much of, and our dressing was replaced by one of cow-dung, which was equally, possibly more, effective.

The pig was run down and bayed by a dog of mine, and finally killed by natives with spears, after the dog had received several deep gashes. I was again in attendance, but was not present at the death, as the pace was far too hot, even had I not been encumbered with a rifle, which hooked itself on to every branch and creeper in sight. The serval cat did fall a victim to my prowess, but even that was not unaided, for it was shot at night sitting in a tree, having been chivvied there by the same dog. The serval cat is a handsome spotted beast much bigger than a cat, though this particular one was black and was an unusual example of melanism.

Living alone on a farm in its early stages of development allowed of few holidays. On a farm 'the master's eye is worth a cartload of dung,' but preaching the gospel of hard work to fifty or more natives day after day was an uphill task, and the time soon arrived when the sight of a boy turned one's stomach. Very likely my presence had the same effect on them, and it was then time to go away for a few days.

The nearest hunting-ground was the Mau Forest, the home of bush buck, elephant, buffalo, the rarely seen bongo, and the giant forest hog. It was only three days' march away, and the difficulties of the ground, the wariness of the game, and the wetness of the climate, made it a place where anything that was bagged was fully earned. Needless to say, little was bagged; all that I can claim in some half-dozen visits are three bush buck. But it was a fascinating place, possessing all the attractiveness of the unknown. It was unsurveyed, and its innermost recesses were known only to a few Wanderobo—thought by some to be the aboriginal inhabitants of the country—though many of the Wanderobo are now natives who have left their own tribes to live in the forest to be free from the restraints of tribal customs. They depend for food on seeds, roots, wild honey, and whatever they can snare or kill.

One might walk, or rather crawl, quietly and stealthily through bamboo thickets, beds of giant nettles, and dripping undergrowth, or perhaps follow warily the broad track stamped out by an elephant, from dawn to dark, seeing no living thing, and hearing nothing but the distant chatter of a monkey or the cry of a hornbill. Another time, a bongo might offer a chance too fleeting to take, or a herd of buffalo would stampede with a fearful crash while one crouched, rooted to the spot, in a tangle of bush too thick to see through; or one followed all day a herd of elephant, looking for the shootable bull which was not there. It is a curious thing that, though elephants were hardly ever shot in the Mau, where, in consequence, shootable bulls should have been numerous, I never saw even so much as the spoor of anything but cows and immature bulls. The local Lumbwa had a story of some fabulous monster of a bull elephant which roamed the Mau, whose tusks were so long and heavy that he was unable to raise them clear of the ground, but they were never able to show me the tracks, surely unmistakable, of this father of all elephants. The natives of most districts where there are elephants have similar tales to tell.

The forest had a great attraction for the Lumbwa, the local natives, who are not merely drawers of water and hewers of wood, but who are fully endowed with the instincts of the hunter and the warrior. The leopard incident was typical of them, and in the spacious days of raid and counter-raid they are said to have given even the Masai as good as they got. They enjoyed exercising their skill as trackers; they found roots and barks, valuable as medicines, which could be obtained only in the Mau; there were choice bamboos for making bows and quivers; and lastly there was always the chance, however remote, of meat.

And so for trips to the forest they were useful allies, except for an ineradicable prejudice against the carrying of loads. Most African natives—that is, all except the pastoral tribes—will carry a load of 50 lbs. or 60 lbs. on their heads and make no bones about it. But the Lumbwa, although agriculturists, are at heart aristocratic stockowners, and refuse to burden themselves with loads. As a favour they will carry up to 20 lbs., but even this must be carried under the arm or on the shoulder as though it were merely a parcel. Their women, perforce, will carry enormous loads, but the men of the tribe are warriors and will not so far demean themselves. Indeed, I think had it been to a place less attractive to them than the forest, or to anywhere where they might have been seen by the men of some other tribe, they would not have consented to carry even 20 lbs.

The forest then was handy, and offered great rewards, but in it the shooting, or rather hunting, was of the sort that would only appeal to the experienced connoisseur, to whom the difficulties to be overcome are more important than the prize. For more fun and less work, for seeing game in vast numbers, for plenty of meat, for hides to make into 'reims'* and yoke-strops, and for the chance of a lion, we had to go further afield. What we termed loosely 'the Plains' was only a small portion of a vast area stretching for hundreds of miles along the Kenya-Tanganyika border. It is the home of the wandering Masai, with their hundreds of thousands of head of cattle; it carries, perhaps, more game to the square mile than anywhere else in the world, so that undoubtedly it is the place for the man who wants to 'shoot' rather than 'hunt.' More interesting by far, and where, after one trip to the Plains, we always went, was the country lying between the Kisii Hills and the beginning of the Plains proper—broken bush country, where the game was less numerous and more difficult to get, but where the possibilities of surprise lurked behind every bush and in every donga.

---

*   Raw hide thongs.

The Plains had the advantage of being easily reached and easily traversed. There we could take a light cart pulled by six oxen in charge of a couple of boys, and wander anywhere at will. It was possible to travel with a cart in the bush country, but movement was restricted to where the cart could go, and, if the best ground was to be reached, porters had to be taken as well—an unfortunate necessity this, because they had to be fed, which task of feeding them was an ever-present threat to our peace of mind. We carried some maize meal for them, but relied largely upon supplementing it with meat; and how the beggars grumbled if large and frequent supplies of it were not forthcoming, and how we hated the job of getting it!

Shooting while on the march, however favourable the opportunity, is not advisable, because it means generally that the march comes to a sudden end, the porters insisting on camping at the kill. Having reached our destination, therefore, one of us, attended by the hungry horde, would have to go out and shoot something. A moderate shot at all times, I found that, when followed by an expectant crowd, the little proficiency I had was sadly impaired. It was rather like a nervous and unskilful golfer driving off in front of a critical swarm of caddies, but there the audience are entirely disinterested as to the result of the shot, while here the case was far otherwise. It was not really vital whether our men stuffed themselves with meat or not, though it did keep them in good heart and enabled them to do long marches, but anxiety to get the job over, and, perhaps, to impress them with the deadliness of the white man's rifle, commonly resulted in some very poor shooting. I had a fellow-feeling for prehistoric man, whose life, with that of his family, depended on his hunting prowess. It must have been a wearing, hand-to-mouth existence, though, no doubt, the hard alternative of success or starvation, kill or die, would have a remarkably beneficial effect on one's abilities. 'Depend upon it, Sir, when a man knows he is to be hanged, it concentrates his mind wonderfully,' was the opinion of Dr Johnson.

If the presence of these expectant mouths waiting to be filled had no good effect upon myself, the effect it had upon our quarry was positively bad. The porters we took on these longer excursions were not natural hunters like the Lumbwa, but men of the Kavirondo tribe, who more than fulfil the popular notion of what an African should be. Jet black, muscular, with squash nose and full lips, clumsy, cheerful, and noisy—all flashing teeth and loud-voiced talk. They had no idea of moving quietly or of making themselves inconspicuous. They would maintain a running commentary in their quiet conversational tone— that is to say, much louder than I could shout—and would gesticulate wildly with both arms to draw my attention to some buck long after I had seen it myself.

Under such conditions a stalk was out of the question, and the shot had to be taken at much longer range than is desirable for clean shooting. The buck, whatever it was, or zebra, if hit, was probably not killed, and would only be brought to bag after a long chase lasting possibly till dark accompanied by a fusillade of shots that disturbed all the game for miles around. Such experiences, the antithesis of good sport, disgusted by their clumsiness and cruelty, but the porters cared nothing about that so long as they got their meat. Great was the rejoicing when this was assured, and the man who grumbled loudly at carrying 50 lbs. along a good path in broad daylight, would stumble home in the dark under a load of 80 lbs. of meat with the best will in the world.

While one of us was performing this unpleasant duty, the other was free to take a quiet stroll with a shot-gun to spy out the land, to look for the fresh spoor of some larger game, or to pick up some unconsidered trifle for our own table. Most of the buck, and even zebra, are good eating, while for the porters size is the criterion, not quality; but for ourselves we preferred a tasty guinea-fowl or pigeon, or the delicious meat of one of the smaller antelopes like duiker, dik-dik, or reedbuck.

We were not always thinking of our own stomachs, or even those of the porters, to the exclusion of everything else, as the foregoing might seem to imply. On our first safari to the bush country our ambitious hopes were fixed upon an elephant. At that time the cost of a licence was less than it is at present, and the value of the ivory more, so that the one balanced the other, while an elephant with good tusks more than paid expenses. The restrictions, however, with which a licence to shoot an elephant was hedged about were so many that, when we came into close contact with our first herd, we were more worried by the legal aspects than by the elephants. No cow elephant could be shot, and only those bulls carrying tusks of over 30 lbs. weight each, while

the penalty for infringing these conditions was the forfeiture of the
ivory and the licence.

We followed the fresh tracks of a small herd, eventually coming
up with them in long, ten to twelve feet high grass—elephant grass, as
it is called. Dotted here and there were flat-topped thorn-trees, from
the top of which we had our only chance of seeing our quarry. Even
from that vantage-point only the tops of their heads and great backs
showed above the sea of grass like a whale breaking the surface. To
our inexperienced eyes it was difficult enough to tell cows from bulls,
much more so to judge the ivory, whose presence was only betrayed by
an occasional gleam of white.

What with fear of the elephants and fear of the Game Laws,
we suffered a deal of nervous wear and tear while we barged about
submerged in the grass sea or watched expectantly from the branch
of some thorn-tree, bitten the while by ferocious tree ants. How we
avoided blundering into or being charged by some peevish cow, or,
through sheer nervousness, shooting some undersized beast, remains
to me a mystery. In the end we had to give it up without ever having
had a view sufficiently clear to justify a shot.

Plodding despondently homewards, as we won clear of the long
grass, we were astonished by the sight of a few stragglers evidently
on the way to join the herd. They were moving slowly up the opposite bank of a small stream, and, with respect for the Game Laws still
uppermost in our minds, we took up a post of observation some fifty
yards from where they would pass. It was fascinating to watch them
gliding along so quietly and majestically; to see one pause, put up his
trunk to wrench off a great branch from some overhanging tree, strip
off and stow away pieces of bark and leaves, drop the peeled branch,
and move on again. Then a cow would pass, shepherding her calf in
front of her with none too playful taps of her trunk.

There was nothing of outstanding size amongst them, but an obvious bull came to a stand right opposite us, broadside on, offering a
perfect target. 'We do it wrong, being so majestical; to offer it the show
of violence,' was certainly how we felt about it, but he seemed war-
rantable, and I had with me a new heavy rifle which I was itching to
try on something worthy of its weight. One shot between eye and ear
dropped him stone dead, leaving us aghast at the suddenness of it and

feeling like murderers with an 'outsize' corpse on our hands. Now that the irrevocable deed was done we were less confident that the ivory was up to the required standard.

The disposal of the body was taken out of our hands by the porters and other natives, men, women, and children, armed with knives, and baskets for the spoil, who seemed to drop out of the sky like so many vultures, possessing, like them, the same uncanny instinct for a corpse. There and then they lit fires and signified their intention of camping on the spot until the meat was finished. Elephant meat is held in high esteem by most natives, who have a belief that by eating it in sufficient quantity they will acquire something of the animal's strength and stature. The cutting up and the subsequent scramble were a revolting sight, frequent fights taking place *inside* the body for the titbits. We had read somewhere that the foot and the best end of the trunk were considered delicacies, but the two nostril holes running through the round of trunk which later appeared on the table were altogether too life-like for the squeamish, while the foot was of exactly that texture and toughness one would expect of a pad of flesh which has to receive and absorb the jar of several tons. Perhaps it had not been hung long enough.

The following day we cut out the tusks. On the ground they looked far more imposing than in the elephant's head, the reason being that a third of the length is embedded in the skull. The part inside the head is hollow, but the size of the hollow decreases until, near the tip, the tusk is solid; the older the elephant the greater is the solid part. We were still rather worried about the weight, and, having no spring balance with us, we were constantly picking them up and balancing them against an imaginary 30 lbs. When finally weighed, they went nearly 50 lbs. each, so that I was able to keep them, but it was nothing to shout about, for a good average pair would go 70 lbs., while tusks of 100 lbs. are still obtainable. The biggest tusk known is in the Natural History Museum, Kensington, and weighs 226½ lbs., and is ten feet long. A large African bull elephant stands over eleven feet at the shoulder, and weighs about six tons.

On the hills of those parts there were, besides elephants, one or two herds of buffalo. These beasts, however, are so wary that you have to be very skilful or lucky, sometimes both, in order to get one. Except in the very early morning and late evening, they seldom leave the shelter of the bush or forest in which most of the day is spent. Day after day we left camp long before the eastern sky had begun to pale, but never did we bring anything back to breakfast except a raging hunger. Whether the buffalo in question had any inkling of our murderous intentions is doubtful, but that they had a profound contempt for us the following regrettable incident seemed to show.

We had at length tired of these fruitless peep-o'-day excursions, and given orders to our Lumbwa cook to be called at a more civilised hour next morning. Imagine, then, our wrath when at the very same time, a full hour before dawn, the wretched boy came creeping into the tent where we slept. We were both awake instantly, but before the storm broke, while we collected our thoughts and sought for words violent enough to express them, the rash youth held up a warning hand and whispered the single word 'Mbogu.' Cautious and hurried whispering elicited the information that the buffalo herd was grazing almost in the camp. Apparently a boot thrown out of the tent could not fail to hit one, and, luckily, the porters were too petrified to stir.

My first thoughtless impulse was to strike a match, but B., hearing me fumbling, hastily stopped me. Then I remembered that my heavy rifle had been taken down to be packed away in its case, and that the only ammunition handy was soft-nosed. (A buffalo has a very tough hide, so that to make sure of sufficient penetration it is advisable to use a solid bullet—that is, a bullet encased in nickel—whereas the soft-nosed bullet has the soft lead tip uncovered.) The same thought had evidently struck B., for he was on the floor, routing about in the haversack which contained his ammunition, cursing softly but vehemently. Afterwards I learnt what the trouble was. B. had false teeth, which in the dark and confusion he had mislaid, and he was now trying to distinguish between solid and soft-nosed bullets in the dark, without being able to bite them.

Finally he got outside, armed, if not to the teeth, at any rate sufficiently, but his diatribes, my oaths, and our dilatoriness had disgusted our callers, and they were gone. We dressed and followed, but it was no use; we had lost our chance. Had our Lumbwa esquire been a Sancho Panza he would no doubt have observed:

'When they bring you the heifer be ready with the rope.'

This humiliation quite spoiled our trip. B. could not, so to speak, get his teeth out of his head, while my well-meant reminders of the seaman's rule, 'A place for everything and everything in its place,' did nothing to solace him. No doubt we had been over-cautious, for at such close quarters any bullet—possibly a charge of buck-shot—would have sufficed.

A very dense strip of bush along the banks of a big river in these parts exercised on me a sinister attraction. It was a veritable warren—not for rabbits, but for rhinos. For hard work coupled with fearful excitement, a few hours in the rhino warren took a lot of beating. The bush was so dense that ingress and progress were only possible by following game tracks, and, once inside, visibility was restricted to a few yards. In such a place, if following tracks, it was almost impossible to keep the wind right, and usually the only warning of the close proximity of a rhino would be an appalling, explosive splutter, like the sound of some gigantic soda syphon in action. There might be a fleeting glimpse of a great grey bulk before the noise of his crashing flight receded in the distance, leaving the hot silence of the bush again undisturbed but for the buzz of a fly and the beating of one's own heart. We never got a shot, and a little of that sort of thing went a long way, but it was a satisfying moment for me when, in a cooler but equally thick place, I dropped a forest rhino at ten yards' range with one shot from a little .256 rifle. Forest rhinos have much longer horns than their fellows of the Plains; this one had a front horn of thirty-six inches. A rhino weighs about three tons, but a shell from a six-inch gun could not have been more deadly than that tiny bullet.

One of these same bush rhinos gave us a night almost as agitated as the night of the buffalo, but him we had no wish to kill even had it been possible, for it was too dark to shoot. We were camped near a water-hole, and, foolishly enough, right astride a very obvious well-used rhino path. About midnight the camp was roused by the familiar sound of the giant soda syphon going off: an alarming sound at all times, in spite of its familiarity, but much more so at night. Some unknown hero from the porters' tent went out to blow up the dying fire while we lit our lamp. Neither had any effect. The most alarming snorts and stampings continued to outrage the peace of an African night.

B. and I took the precaution of loading our rifles, but it was raining, we could see nothing, so we remained in bed—unwisely, I thought, because if the rhino did decide to charge through the camp to reach the water-hole, he would very likely vent his fury on the tent in passing. Rhinos have very poor eyesight, so that the tent would have offered the most tempting target. It was comforting to reflect that the porters' tent was bigger than ours. Meantime, they were very unhappy, and one by one they piled into our tent for moral support, and B.'s dog, a big Rampur greyhound, had all his hackles up but was far too frightened to bark. There was nothing we could do. Our combined voices could not have produced a noise equal to the rhino's, or one that would have any intimidating effect. Indeed, shouting was an experiment we did not care to try, as it might have had the opposite effect. So we just sat still, and at each explosion of the perambulating syphon I smiled a wan and sickly smile.

We endured this unhappy situation for a tense hour, until it apparently dawned on the angry, spluttering rhino that a slight deviation from his normal route would take him to the water without walking through our camp. This he must have done, for we heard no more.

This dog of B.'s—Bruce, as he was called—came to an untimely end soon afterwards. He went off hunting on his own and was never seen again, although we waited for a day to scour the country and to send back to the last camp. Probably a leopard got him. He was not destined for a long life, anyhow, for he was an inveterate sheep-killer, and, in a country where every native owned sheep and goats, and in those days usually carried a spear, it was a wonder that no one had put a spear into him before this. Still, he was a great loss to B., for he was a handsome dog, with some very endearing ways. You had only to say to him: 'Laugh, Bruce,' and he would bare his teeth and wrinkle up his nose in a dreadful grin. Less amusing was a trick he had of stealing food. My house was nearly two miles from B.'s, but very often Bruce would come over in the night, break open my ramshackle larder, and treat himself to a snack of a couple of loaves and a dozen eggs. Peace to his memory, for at least he lived dangerously!

Returning home from these excursions, it was exciting to see how the flax had grown, or how the last planting of young coffee seedlings had 'taken,' but we had, invariably, to steel our minds against the recital of a chapter of accidents by the head boy whom we had left in charge; the oxen that had strayed or died, the boys that had deserted; how the plough had broken the day we left, and had done no work since. So ran the tale, while other less obvious items, such as disease in the cattle or the coffee, we had the fun of finding out later for ourselves.

Perhaps, when I mentioned a fiver as our total outlay for these expeditions, I was underestimating, and, on looking backwards and taking into account that which was done and more that was not done in our absence, I suspect that this was so. But, whatever the cost, it was money well spent.

CHAPTER III

KILIMANJARO:
KIBO AND MAWENZI

So, and no otherwise hillmen desire their hills.

—Kipling

A T FIRST SIGHT few places would appear to offer less scope for mountaineering than tropical Africa—mountaineering, that is, in the full sense of the word; by which I mean climbing on ice, snow, and glaciers, as well as rock. But in fact there are three widely separated regions where such climbing is to be had; in two of them on isolated peaks, and in the third on a range of snow peaks. In the course of the next few years, by taking full advantage of the working agreement reached at the end of Chapter I, and by meeting someone of a like mind to myself, who had as yet also escaped being 'shut up,' I was able to visit all three.

Kilimanjaro, 19,710 feet, is an extinct volcano lying about 180 miles south-east of Nairobi, just inside the Tanganyika border. The boundary between Kenya and Tanganyika, which is elsewhere a straight line, bulges out to the north to include Kilimanjaro in Tanganyika Territory, or German East Africa, as it was when the boundary was delineated. The story is commonly related (and, whether true or not, it has too firm a hold now to be given up) that when the boundary was fixed according to the Treaty of 1890, Kilimanjaro was specifically included in Germany territory, at the cost of an unstraight line, so that the German Emperor might have the gratification of possessing the highest mountain in Africa.

It was first seen in 1848 by the two missionaries Rebmann and Krapf, and was climbed for the first time by Hans Mayer and Ludwig Purtscheller in 1889. High though it is and capped with ice and snow descending as low as 16,000 feet on the south-west and to 18,500 feet on the north side, the great bulk of the mountain is more impressive than its height, for to travel round the base would involve a journey on foot of several days. The enormous base detracts from the apparent height, and this detraction is accentuated by the squat, pudding-like dome of Kibo, the highest summit. In fine weather Kibo can be seen from Nairobi, when the haze rising from the hot intervening plains blots out the lower slopes, leaving the white dome suspended in mid-air like a cloud. The Masai, who inhabit the plains between Nairobi and the mountain, call Kibo 'Ngaje Ngai'—the House of God.

On the last day of February 1930, S. and I forgathered at Nairobi, whence we left by car for the mountain. S. who, like myself, was a coffee planter, had a farm north of the railway about 160 miles from mine. In the middle of it was a great tooth of granite, which soared up for about 200 feet—an eyesore to a planter, but to those of the Faith better than water in a thirsty land. S. had worked out several routes up it to which I was later introduced.

From Nairobi the road runs south through the Southern Game Reserve—vast plains, sparsely dotted with thorn-trees a few feet high, and at this season of the year, towards the end of the dry weather, burnt almost bare of grass. Nevertheless, these plains support great quantities of game, together with two or three hundred thousand head of Masai cattle. These Masai are pastoral nomads, who in former days overran the whole of East Africa, but are now confined to their Reserve, which includes part of the Game Reserve. They number only about 22,000, and, since they have at their disposal over 200 acres per head, there is room for them, their cattle, and the game. All the land, of course, is not equally good, but they follow the best grazing according to the season. They live in low huts of hides plastered with cow-dung, built contiguously in the form of a circle, inside of which the cattle are put at night for safety from lions, and, in former days, hostile tribes. The Masai village, or *manyatta*, inevitably becomes in a short time a quagmire of trampled mud and cow-dung, infested with myriads of flies. The diet of the Masai consists almost exclusively of blood and milk, the blood being obtained by bleeding their cattle. They do no work except tend their herds and flocks, and they have the frank manner and

Kilimanjaro: The main crater in 1933; much less snow than normally

Kilimanjaro: Another view of the crater in 1933

independent bearing that befit such a life. Although clean in person, they live in the utmost squalor, have no morals as understood by us, and are complete savages; but their bravery is proverbial, and they are savages of a rather glorious type.

The road across the plains was at that time more or less as nature had made it. Little improvement had been attempted except to put 'Irish' bridges across the sandy beds of the water-courses. These take the form of a concrete causeway across the beds of the numerous dongas, which for most of the year are dry, but which on occasion can become formidable rivers within a matter of minutes. For crossing the sand beds of these dongas when dry, the 'Irish' bridge is most useful, but the way into and out of these river-beds was always a strain on the car and one's nerves; I remember one, where the front wheels started climbing out before the back wheels had finished going down.

The road between these fearsome places was seamed and scored with parallel ruts and transverse cracks, sometimes a foot wide; the pace was therefore circumspect, so that the man who was not driving had leisure to admire the game which was to be seen on either hand. There a rhino would be grazing peacefully two hundred yards from the road; here the head of a giraffe might stare at us superciliously from over the top of a thorn-tree not twenty yards away, before the owner of it glided away in his strange, undulating gallop; and once we stopped the car to inspect through field-glasses a lion lying under a bush a quarter of a mile from the road. When we got out in order to go closer, he got up and walked away with his tail twitching contemptuously.

We reached Longido (130 miles) after dark, and stopped there for the night. There was a rest house, and hard by is Mount Longido, a conical scrub-covered hill rising straight from the plain to a height of 8500 feet. It was the scene of heavy fighting at the commencement of the War in East Africa in 1914.

Next day a run of 120 miles over a better road took us to Marungu, a little place on the south-east slopes of the mountain at an elevation of about 5000 feet above the sea. We had driven round two sides of the mountain—the west and south sides—on which there is a considerable area devoted to coffee-growing by both natives and Europeans. The volcanic soil is deep and rich, the climate warm, while water furrows can be led everywhere from the innumerable streams descending from the forested slopes of the mountain above. At Marungu there is a small hotel where we put up, dumped our surplus kit, and arranged for twelve porters and a donkey to accompany us next day.

When the Germans were in occupation here they built two huts on the mountain; one at 8500 feet, which is called Bismarck, and another at 11,500 feet, called Peters's Hut, after Dr Karl Peters, the notorious German explorer, whose efforts to extend the German sphere of influence to Uganda, when matters there were still undecided, did not stop at opening the private correspondence of his British rivals. These huts, particularly the lower one, are in fairly frequent use by visitors to Marungu, which is popular as a health resort for people condemned to live in hot, unhealthy places like Tanga, on the neighbouring coast. Apart from the great altitude, there is nothing to stop the more energetic from going to the top, because on Kibo there are no climbing difficulties whatsoever. Perhaps that is putting it too strongly, for on any mountain much depends on the weather, and on Kibo in thick weather the finding of the summit presents more difficulties than usual. The reason for this will be apparent later, but, I suppose, up to 1930 at least twenty people had made genuine ascents, and a few others, like ourselves, ascents which were only technically invalid.

Leaving Marungu, the track to Bismarck follows a broad spur at an easy gradient. On every hand are the huts, banana groves, maize and coffee fields of the natives, the lower slopes at this point being thickly populated and well cultivated by the Wachagga, who seem to have a good working knowledge of the art of irrigation. At about 7000 feet the cultivation comes to an end on the fringes of the forest zone. Inside the forest it is dark and gloomy; the undergrowth is thick; streams abound, and the trees are typical of those found in 'rain forest.' These are evergreen, the species numerous, trees of all sizes and shapes struggling together for space and light. Elephants abound, but are protected, and near the Bismarck hut their tracks lie everywhere, making the finding of the path to the hut difficult.

This is a substantial structure of stone situated near the upper limit of the forest zone. Little more than four hours were needed to reach it, and that evening, after we had settled in, we climbed to a point clear of the forest to enjoy a good view of Mawenzi, a fantastically weathered peak of red volcanic rock, 17,000 feet high, separated from the higher but less interesting Kibo by a wide, flat saddle of shale. It looked difficult, and, if the climbing of Kibo was a duty, that of Mawenzi promised to be a pleasure.

Rain fell heavily in the night, but we got away soon after seven to a fine morning, and reached Peters's Hut in four hours, just in time to avoid a sharp hailstorm. The path lay over bare and boggy moors, where we saw for the first time the curious plants peculiar to the Alpine zone in the tropics. This zone lies between 10,000 and 14,000 feet, and the most remarkable plants found there are the giant groundsel and the giant lobelia. The first is like an enormous cabbage stuck on top of a thick stem six to eight feet high, while the lobelia is a long, columnar, feathery, green stalk, very unlike an ordinary lobelia. Besides these there are Alpines, balsams, heather-like bushes, and withal many more birds than are seen in the rather lifeless forest.

The hut was a small wooden building with a tin roof and a very efficient stove, for which we had brought a supply of wood. Not unreasonably, the porters, whose quarters were distinctly airy, complained bitterly of the cold, while the little white donkey voiced the sentiments of all with a series of discordant brays, and looked very much out of place. The walls of the hut were sadly disfigured by the names of the many parties who had penetrated thus far, and who were not willing to have it forgotten.

In the night there was a heavy thunderstorm, and, judging from the solid banks of cloud below and to the south, we feared that the 'long rains' were about to break. The rainy season generally sets in towards the end of March—slightly earlier, perhaps, in Tanganyika than in Kenya, because the rain spreads up from the south with the advance of the south-west monsoon. This unusually early onset of the rains foreboded for us not only unpleasant conditions on the mountain, but the possibility of getting stranded on the way home by rivers in flood.

Nearing the 16,000-foot saddle, and within a mile of the hut, we came upon snow. Our head porter and guide, one Solomon, who had been very near to the top of Kibo, if not on it, pointed out our destination, the Hans Mayer Caves, across the saddle. It looked about half a mile distant, but it took us an hour to get there, and we realised the height was beginning to tell. The porters, who were anxious to dump their loads and get back from these inhospitable wastes to the comparative comfort of Peters's Hut, went well, and we did our best, but our little white dapple had the legs and lungs of us all.

The cave, like most caves, still seemed to be the home of many winds unreleased by Æolus, but we made ourselves fairly comfortable, and prepared for an early start next day. I had a slight headache, due to the altitude, but S. was fit enough. The donkey and all the porters had gone down except Solomon and one companion, who suffered together silently. There is nothing, I think, except cold which will reduce an African native to speechlessness, and that unusual state of affairs is perhaps accounted for by the impossibility of talking intelligibly with chattering teeth.

We started at 4.30 a.m. in thick weather and falling snow. The route at first lay up snow lying thinly on scree at an easy angle. The climb is devoid of interest from a mountaineering point of view, so the reader is, for the moment, spared the arduous mental exertion of following the party up the perilous knife-edge ridges, stone-swept gullies, and precipitous faces which abound so plentifully in descriptions of a climb. On top of Kilimanjaro is a great flat-bottomed crater, possibly a mile across at its longest diameter, filled with ice and snow—what the Germans called on their map the Credner Glacier. On the rim of the crater is the summit, or summits, for on this great circumference there are numerous snow hillocks or bumps of varying height. The rim is gained by a notch at its lowest point, which is close on 19,000 feet, and then the climber turns left-handed to follow the crater-wall round to the south and west, passing over several of these bumps, until the highest of all, Kaiser Wilhelm Spitze, is reached.

At half past ten we gained the first of these points, Gillman Point, in a mist, where, digging in the snow, we found a cairn and a visitors' book. Solomon, with the wisdom of his namesake, now declared he had had enough, so we parked him there to await our return, and pushed on, well knowing that the official summit was still far off, though very little higher. I was not feeling very well myself; in fact I was being sick at frequent intervals; but we ploughed slowly on through waist-deep snow, presently reaching the top of another bump, which later we judged must have been Stella Point. Yet another top loomed

Kilimanjaro: Leopard's Point, and crater wall behind; the dessicated body of the leopard can be seen on the top of the rock (left foreground)

vaguely through the mists some distance ahead, but I am obliged to confess that its challenge aroused little interest in us, and, after debate, we turned in our tracks. We picked up the patient Solomon, now the colour of a mottled and overripe Victoria plum, and at twelve o'clock started down.

When a party fails to get to the top of a mountain, it is usual and convenient to have some picturesque excuse—preferably some objective reason for turning back, such as the dangerous state of the snow, the approach of bad weather, or falling stones, so that a story of failure makes better reading than one of success, while a chorus of praise resounds to the party's display of sound judgment and its unselfish renunciation of a victory easily within its grasp. If the story of our failure has lost something in the telling, it is owing to an unfortunate propensity, perhaps only temporary, for truth, and the reason for our retreat was the more prosaic and not uncommon one—inability to go any further.

During our flounderings in the vicinity of the summit the weather was so thick and the sun so effectually hidden that we had both discarded our snow-glasses, the better to see where we were going. When we got back to the cave about two o'clock our eyes began to smart, then to hurt, until by evening they were firmly closed and exceedingly painful. We were completely snow-blind. The pain made the night a wretched one, but by morning our eyes were on the mend. It snowed all that day, during which we slept, pottered about near the cave, and discussed our next move... A stern sense of duty prompted some half-hearted talk of finishing what we now suspected was the uncompleted task of climbing Kibo, but the fresh snow which had fallen, and the bad weather, gave us a good excuse for going down to the warmth and comfort of Peters's Hut. No one was more delighted at this decision than the faithful Solomon, though it would be idle to pretend that we ourselves acted upon it with any great show of reluctance.

It was raining hard when we arrived there at noon next day, which so disgusted us that we almost abandoned hope of Mawenzi, and talked of retreat from the mountain. However, that evening the weather appeared more promising, so we decided to wait.

March 8th, however, was another day of mist and rain. At night there was another violent thunderstorm, but, rendered desperate by inactivity, we resolved to attempt Mawenzi next day, be the weather what it might.

The two of us left the hut at 3.15 a.m. and reached the saddle between Kibo and Mawenzi soon after dawn... At least, we assumed the slight lessening of the gloom was the dawn, for a dense mist shrouded everything, and we sat there waiting for a clearing to disclose the whereabouts of our peak. This was presently vouchsafed us, and at eight o'clock we were sitting at the foot of the north-west face of Mawenzi waiting impatiently for another clearing to give us some hint as to where to start. No clearing came, so we roped up and began poking about tentatively at the foot of the rocks. The peak had been climbed twice before, and we were looking for a couloir which was the key to the ascent. We entered a chimney which looked invitingly simple, but were soon brought to a stand and an ignominious retreat by the ice and snow with which the rocks were plastered.

This check seemed to rouse us from our defeatist attitude, just as an insult may goad the most placid into determined activity. We dumped our rucksacks at the foot and started again, and at nine o'clock we reached the foot of a promising-looking gully. The whole mountain was iced, the rock rotten, snow falling, and it was still misty, but in defiance of these bad conditions we continued the climb. Four short rock pitches divided by stretches of steep snow landed us at the foot of a subsidiary gully coming down from the left. This seemed to be the line of least resistance, so we turned up it, and, after a severe struggle, reached the top of one of the several jagged teeth which decorate the summit ridge. The time was about two o'clock. We could now see that it was not the highest of them, for this lay at the head of the main gully. It is called Wissmann Spitze on the German map. Descending rapidly into the main gully, we climbed a steep snow slope, and gained the summit at four o'clock.

No view but the half-seen snows of Kibo greeted us, but now, as ever, the joy of difficulties overcome was ample reward. We had no time to waste, and hastily began the descent, where, in the course of climbing down one of the rock pitches via S.'s shoulders, I lost both hat and snow-glasses, which went spinning down the gully. We reached the foot of the rocks before dark, and, not stopping to look for my property, raced down the 3000 feet to Peters's in the gathering gloom, fearful lest we should miss the hut.

Breakfast at Bismarck, lunch at Marungu, marks the rapidity of our retreat next day. We paid off and dismissed the porters; Solomon, wise as ever, forgetting to return a heavy overcoat which S. had lent him. Our fears about the effect of the early rains upon the road were fully confirmed, and we learnt that the direct road to Nairobi was now impassable. The only alternative was to follow the old Mombasa road east via Taveta to Voi on the railway, 200 miles the wrong side of Nairobi and only 100 miles from Mombasa. From there we could try the new road which follows roughly the alignment of the railway, or, if the worst came, go back by train.

All went well as far as Voi, which was reached in one day without incident. Trouble began next morning at a river, where the bridge, only an 'Irish' one, had been washed away. Luckily there were a gang of natives at work on the road, who pushed us across the fifty yards of flooded river while the water swirled over the floorboards of the car. We bowled merrily along a road on which lay many pools. These we took as they came at full speed, careful trials having assured us that the bottoms were hard. At midday we had the misfortune to encounter one that refused to be rushed. It was deep and soft, and the car settled down with the back axle sitting firmly on the ridge between the ruts, while the wheels revolved helplessly in a liquid mud bath of nauseous colour and smell. All the usual expedients of jacking up, digging out, and strewing branches were tried, without any result but to plaster us in mud from head to foot. There was nothing to be done but wait upon the event, and presently a lorry came along and pulled us out of the slough. Proceeding with more caution, we reached that night Makindu, a station on the railway, where we heard that ahead of us there were a dozen cars and lorries waiting for a flooded river to subside. At that time the Mombasa-Nairobi road was very popular with transport agents, the Government having been foolishly persuaded to spend some money on making it passable. This resulted in a serious loss of traffic to the railway (a familiar story), but the *status quo ante* was speedily restored when the Government withheld funds for the road's upkeep, allowing it to revert to its former state. S. was in a hurry to get home, so boarded the train next morning, while I arranged for an open truck to receive the much-enduring car—a necessary arrangement, but one that seriously upset the expedition's balance-sheet. I ran the car on to the truck, but we did not get hitched on to a goods train until evening. We chugged away through the night, myself sitting in the car, too cold to sleep, and imagining I was back in the draughty cave on Kibo. When dawn came we were running across the Plains we had traversed a short fortnight ago: then, bare brown veldt, now a fresh green carpet on which the drifting herds of game grazed contentedly, hardly deigning to watch our dragon-like progress.

CHAPTER IV

KENYA MOUNTAIN

Behind that leader, who gave me hope and was a light to me.

—DANTE

THE MOUNTAIN WHICH GIVES its name to the Colony is a magnificent isolated peak rising out of a plain, of a general elevation of 6000 feet, to a height of 17,040 feet. It lies about 130 miles north of Nairobi by road, and within a few miles of the equator. The base of the mountain rivals that of Kilimanjaro in size, the drive round it by road being a journey of over 100 miles. The lower slopes of Kenya are forested, like those of Kilimanjaro, and both are extinct volcanoes, but there the likeness ends, for the two summits are as different as the dome of St. Paul's and the spire of Salisbury. This illustration is only used to emphasise the contrast; the dome of St. Paul's would pass as a likeness to Kibo, but there is nothing spire-like about the peak of Kenya. Rather is it a great jagged tower, buttressed by a number of equally jagged ridges, while between the ridges the rock faces of the tower are festooned with snow and hanging glaciers.

The mountain is a very old volcano, judged by geologists to have been at one time 3000 feet higher. No trace of the original crater remains, while the peak itself consists of the rock which in past ages consolidated into a 'plug' and sealed up the volcano. This rock is of a peculiar type which was given the name 'kenyte' by the late Professor Gregory, after whom one of the glaciers on Kenya has been named. The same sort of rock has been found on Mount Erebus, in the Antarctic. It is not as reliable as it might be from a climber's point of view, but it is infinitely better than the loose volcanic 'tuffs' found on some of the neighbouring lesser peaks, such as Sendeyo, whose rock is similar to the rock of Mawenzi. There are a dozen named glaciers, but some are only small hanging glaciers, while none are to be compared for size with Alpine glaciers.

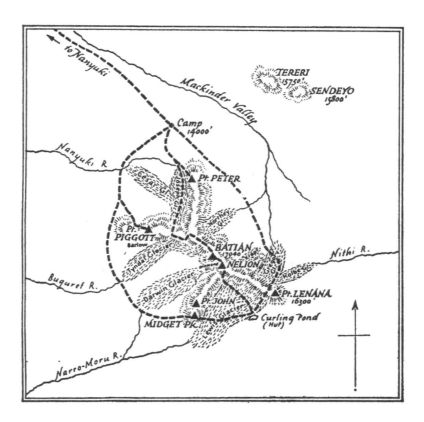

Map 2: Mount Kenya

The peak was first seen in 1849 by Dr Krapf, a German working for a British missionary society. His story was received in Europe with incredulity, for at that time the existence of snow mountains in equatorial Africa was regarded by many as an impossibility. Already, in November 1849, Krapf had seen Kilimanjaro, and in December of the same year he writes from Kitui, 'I could see the "Kegnia" more distinctly, and observed two large horns or pillars, as it were, rising over an enormous mountain to the north-west of Kilimanjaro, covered with a white substance.'

Fifty years passed before it was climbed by Sir Halford Mackinder and his two Alpine guides, César Oilier and Joseph Brocherel, in 1899. This feat was the more remarkable when it is remembered that the railway to Nairobi was only under construction, that the tribes between there and the mountain were in a very unsettled state, and that food-supplies had to be brought up from Naivasha, fifty miles away. The summit is crowned by twin peaks to which Mackinder gave the names of Batian and Nelion. Batian, which is the higher by about forty feet, Mackinder's party climbed direct, omitting Nelion altogether. The climb from their high camp to the summit, a matter of 2000 feet, took six hours, and a like time was spent on the descent.

It was another thirty years before the second successful attempt was made, though many parties had tried. In 1929 Messrs. Shipton and Wyn Harris reached the summit of Batian, having first traversed over the top of Nelion. Their route followed that of Mackinder's up the south-east face of Nelion, but on nearing the lower summit Mackinder's party had traversed beneath it and across the steep, tough ice of the hanging Diamond Glacier, whereas the later party took Nelion in their stride. The new route involved difficult rock climbing, but that would be preferred by an amateur party to the three hours of step-cutting on steep ice which the traverse of the Diamond Glacier demanded of Mackinder's guides.

The twin peaks were named by Mackinder after the man who was then *laibon*, or chief witch-doctor, of the Masai, and his brother. Batian—or Mbatian, as it should be written—was not only a witch-doctor, but a man of great influence over his tribe, and a prophet. He is said to have prophesied the coming of the white man to Kenya even before Europeans had been there, and another of his prophecies was

Mount Kenya: Pack ponies

Mount Kenya: A cave camp in the Mackinder Valley

that a great snake would come, stretching from the sea right across the land, and with its coming the supremacy of the Masai would cease. The Masai believe that Batian's 'great snake' is the railway. Two lesser peaks are named Sendeyo and Lenana, after Batian's sons, and the story of Batian's death and the disputed inheritance bears a close resemblance to the story of Isaac and Jacob. The brothers and their supporters fought together for many years, until, in 1902, Sendeyo the elder was beaten and sued for peace with Lenana his brother, who had cheated him out of the succession. It was a happy thought of Sir Halford Mackinder's to use names whose music sounds even clearer now amongst the dull cluster of disharmonious European names which have been sprinkled lavishly over the remaining peaks, glaciers, and valleys.

Not long after our return from Kilimanjaro I heard from S. that the coffee had managed so well in his absence that he was now ready to carry out a plan which he had long had in mind. This was nothing less than a traverse of the twin peaks of Kenya by ascending the west ridge and descending by the 1929 route. I was quite agreeable, and, whether we succeeded in carrying out this ambitious plan or not, we expected to put in a very good fortnight playing about on the mountain. This time our rendezvous was Nakuru, a town 100 miles west of Nairobi, where we forgathered towards the end of July. S. brought with him one of his farm boys named Saidi, to cook and make himself generally useful. His normal occupation was driving a tractor.

Nanyuki, our jumping-off place at the foot of the mountain, was 240 miles away, but we were anxious to get there in the day. At least one of us was, for S. was burning with impatience to be on the mountain, while I, who had to drive, would have been content to reach it in two. We left Nakuru at half past four in the morning in rain and mist, and lost some precious time by missing the way in the fog and going for some miles down the wrong road. By the time we had breakfasted at Naivasha the weather had improved, and, as we climbed the steep, rough road up the escarpment out of the Rift Valley, the parched country looked, as was usual there, as though it did not know what rain was.

An hour was spent in Nairobi collecting some food and necessaries, but we left again at midday with 140 miles still to go. It remained dry until we pulled into Nanyuki at six o'clock, but while we were enquiring the whereabouts of the farm from which we had arranged to take transport, there was a heavy shower. The farm was only a mile or two out, but the road to it consisted mainly of two enormous ruts, out of which it was essential to keep the wheels. The rain was fatal to a safe negotiation of this atrocity, and, after several hairbreadth escapes, we landed fairly in both ruts, the car sitting firmly down on the axles. It was almost dark, so we abandoned ship and walked on to the farm, where we slept.

Next morning was a busy one. The car had to be rescued with a team of oxen, and our impedimenta made up into 50 lb. loads, but at one o'clock we started with five pack-ponies, led by six boys, to carry our ten loads. The way led through homely grass glades surrounded by cedar forest, where a rhino, standing in the middle of one, looked as unreal as a dragon would have done. We had to pass within 200 yards of him, but he elected to run away instead of stampeding blindly through the caravan—a contingency that one should always be prepared for in the presence of these eccentric beasts. Having steered safely past this Scylla, we nearly got foul of Charybdis in the shape of a big bull elephant standing at the edge of the forest. The ponies got very jumpy, but he too moved quietly away, and allowed us to settle into our camp just inside the forest. A heavy storm just missed us, so that we spent a happy evening under the cedars sitting round a noble fire. No elephant or rhino came to disturb the peace of the night—a peace which was broken only by the distant snapping of a bamboo, where, perhaps, some elephant moved, and by the slow, shrill, long-drawn cry of the tree hyrax—that unforgettable sound which for me embodies all the mystery and charm of Africa.

Next morning our march continued through the forest zone, the Kikuyu pony-men beating tins and shouting to give timely warning of our approach to any rhino, buffalo, or elephant within earshot. On the west and north side of the mountain, the forest is of a drier type than the 'rain' forest of Kilimanjaro, which is found again on the wetter eastern slopes of Kenya. Cedar-trees predominated amongst olive and podo-carpus; all valuable for timber, but the first-named especially so because it is the pencil cedar.

The trees, growing scanty and stunted, yielded at length to bamboos, which in turn faded away as we reached the beginning of the moors of tussocky grass, heath, and giant groundsel. Here one of the

Mount Kenya: Twin peaks of Mount Kenya from Mackinder Valley, showing
giant groundsel in the foreground

ponies had to be relieved of its load, and, before we reached the caves
which were our objective, everyone was tired and the boys mutinous.
The cave which the natives annexed was very good; ours was wet; but
there was no lack of groundsel, which makes an excellent fuel.

In the night two of the ponies ran away, so that some reorganisa-
tion was needed before we got away at half past ten with three ponies,
one of which I now led, while S. and three of the boys carried the
remaining loads. Our way lay up the broad Mackinder Valley, and as
we marched we gazed at the peak, filling the head of the valley and
looking like some glorious cathedral. A cloudless blue sky, with the
sunlight sparkling on the glaciers, gave vigour to the black outlines of
its rock.

We took up our quarters in another convenient cave near the head
of the valley, at a height of about 14,000 feet. Saidi we kept with us, but
the boys and the ponies we sent down to the lower camp with instructions to visit us occasionally for orders. In spite of the height, there was
still plenty of senecio (giant groundsel) for fuel, and it was needed,
because the night was clear and cold, with the thermometer registering
some six degrees of frost.

Our first task was to reconnoitre the west ridge, and to do this we
made ascents of two rock aiguilles of about 16,000 feet. The comfort
and conveniences of our base had to be paid for by a rather laborious
climb up a steep, dry, boulder-strewn watercourse, which had to be
ascended and descended every day going to and returning from the
scene of our activities. The climbing of these two rock peaks, Dutton
and Peter—which, by the way, were first ascents—made a satisfying and
not too difficult first day, and showed us that the west ridge could be
reached from a col at its foot. The col lay at the head of the Joseph Glacier, and the problem of reaching it, and the nature of the ridge above
it, were the questions to which we devoted the second day.

Leaving camp at seven, we reached the snout of the glacier at half
past eight. Some step-cutting was necessary to gain a lodgment on the
glacier, up which we then went as far as the foot of an ice couloir leading to our col. Here we took to some rotten and rather difficult rock on
its left bank, and reached the col before midday. The col was narrow,
and sitting astride it, à cheval, we gazed with fascination at the terrific
view of the west face of the mountain. Below the almost vertical cliffs

of the pinnacled west ridge were two hanging glaciers which seemed to cling there in defiance of all laws of gravity. Below them again, the rocks, which were swept by the ice falling from these glaciers, curved steeply to the Tyndall Glacier, a thousand feet below us. The little we could see of the lower part of our proposed route up the ridge was not encouraging. An upward traverse over steep ice and snow-covered rock led to a notch between what we called the Grand and Petit Gendarme, and everything depended on our ability to turn the former by a traverse on the north side, which we could not see, in order to gain the ridge above it. What lay beyond we could not tell, and it seemed doubtful whether we should get far enough to learn.

Sitting on the col, while the mists boiled up and shrouded the ridge from our straining eyes, we debated whether to attack it the next day. We had seen as much of the route as we ever would, steps were cut up to the col and would not last more than a day or two, and the weather seemed settled. The only advantage of delay was to acclimatise more, for, though we now reaped the benefit of the acclimatisation received on Kilimanjaro, we should probably be fitter still after another day or two, and the obvious difficulties of the ridge plus the altitude would call for all our reserves. A natural desire to put it at once to the test carried the day, and we decided to make our bid next morning. It would be August 1st, but, though the fact that this was also S.'s birthday was not given any undue weight, it would be a very nice birthday present if we pulled it off.

We were up at 3 a.m. on this eventful morning, left camp at 4.30 a.m., and were at the foot of the Joseph Glacier at dawn. Our steps were intact, so we mounted rapidly, this time taking to the rocks on the opposite side of the ice couloir, which brought us to the col at a point nearer to the foot of the west ridge. We were there by 8 a.m., and sat on its knife-edge for a breather with our legs dangling over the Tyndall Glacier below.

We roped up and began climbing, with S. leading, as he did from here to the top. The traverse across the south flank of the Petit Gendarme took time and care. The rocks were steep, exposed, and plastered with ice and snow, which had to be chipped or scraped away before foothold could be found on the rock beneath. We moved one at a time, crossing a series of rock ribs which effectually concealed from us what

lay ahead. We liked the whole thing so little that there was some talk
of retreat, but we agreed that we should at least gain the notch before
admitting that we had bitten off more than we could chew.

This was at length reached by an ice couloir just before midday,
when the usual mists began to envelop the peak and the upper part
of our ridge. A halt was called to munch some chocolate before going
on to have a look at the traverse on the north side of the Grand Gendarme. As the rocks on that side were dry and free from snow, and as
the memory of what we had just climbed was fresh in our minds, we
both preferred going on to going back. Some difficult rock had to be
overcome before we succeeded at last in turning the Grand Gendarme
and gaining the ridge once more above it, and twice the leader had
to accept a shoulder from the second man wedged in a crack below.
We were confronted now by a succession of pinnacles, none so imposing as the Grand Gendarme, but one or two gave just as much trouble
to surmount. No turning movement below these was possible, for the
ridge now fell away almost sheer on both sides, so that each had to be
taken as it came.

Snow began falling lightly, but, as this seemed a daily occurrence
of an afternoon, we were not unduly alarmed by it; indeed, so preoc-
cupied were we with the climbing that it passed almost unheeded. We
had now got to the point where the north-east ridge abutted against the
west ridge, which here turns southwards towards the summit, almost
horizontally. Climbing along the crest on unstable rocks, we were presently faced by a great gap in the ridge into which it was impossible to
climb. Conscious that by so doing we were denying ourselves the possibility of retreat, we lowered ourselves down into it.

Crossing the icy crest of the cap, more ridge-work followed, the
rock being now of a hard columnar formation which was very pleasant to handle. A patch of difficult ice just below the summit delayed
but did not stop us, and at 4.15 we climbed, tired but elated, on to
the summit of Batian. Except for the brief halts on the col and below
the Grand Gendarme, we had been climbing continuously for twelve
hours.

S. was familiar with the route down on the south-east side, but there
were a bare two hours of daylight left, so, allowing only time to swallow each a small tin of meat essence, we began the descent. Crossing

the Gate of the Mists between Batian and Nelion, we lost much valuable time by having to cut steps in hard, sticky ice. Nelion was climbed, and, without pause, we started down the other side. Things now began to happen. First the point of my axe was twisted clean off, and then, as I was descending a rock pitch with the axe hitched in the rope round my waist, a slip, which was immediately checked, jerked the axe free and it shot down the slope bound for the Lewis Glacier. At the same time S. was attacked with violent spasms of vomiting, which could only be attributed to the meat essence. Each bout of sickness necessitated a long halt and made him progressively weaker.

Our pace slowed, the light began to fade, and the rocks became almost too cold to handle. A bivouac was suggested, for with one man axeless, one sick, and both tired, it was becoming questionable whether we could continue to climb safely, but a bitter east wind springing up banished all thoughts of a bivouac, and the light of the moon which sailed out from behind some cloud encouraged us to persevere. Very slowly and cautiously we climbed down, using the rope to lower ourselves wherever possible. The most vivid impression that remains in my mind of this grim ordeal is how S., in the feeble state he was, not only climbed, but led the way unerringly and safeguarded his companion.

At about 9 p.m. we descended by means of a final 'rappel' on to the frozen snow of the Lewis Glacier, whence, unroping, we began the trudge up to Point Lenana, a snow ridge which had to be crossed on the way back to our camp some four or five hours' march away. Now that the tension was over we realised how exhausted we were. The gentle slope of hard snow in front of us appeared quite insuperable, and we now remembered that there was a hut lower down the glacier near a place called the Curling Pond. For this we headed, where, on reaching it about 10 p.m., we lay and shivered until the first streak of light encouraged us to start once more for our camp. S.'s sickness had passed off, and we got there by 8 a.m., when we promptly turned in and spent the rest of the day in bed. Our return home with the milk did not seem to surprise the faithful Saidi, nor did he display much curiosity as to what we had been doing since we left camp the previous morning. What did astonish him, I think, was our hunger, which took several days to appease.

Mount Kenya: North face of twin peaks of Mount Kenya (Nelion on left, Batian on right); Northey Glacier is in right centre

This climb took such a lot out of us that little more was done until August 5th, when we climbed Sendeyo, a very striking rock peak on the opposite side of the Mackinder Valley. The rock was volcanic tuff, very hard on the hands, and apt to give way at a severe look. Most advantageously placed for photography as we were, it was disappointing that the mists came down earlier than usual over the main peak and remained down.

On the following day we made a first ascent of Point Piggott, 16,350 feet. It was thus named by Professor Gregory after an officer of the B.E.A. Company who had assisted him in his expedition. Gregory, who visited the mountain in 1892 on a scientific expedition, was the first to reach the glaciers. A glacier was named after him by Mackinder.

Piggott is a peak that is nearly all ridge, a continuation, in fact, of our west ridge, but cut off from the main peak by the col from which we began our climb. The real summit of Piggott lies at the north-east end of the ridge and thus overlooks our col, but it was too steep to tackle from there. We gained the summit ridge further to the west after some difficult climbing, and the summit itself was not reached until 1 p.m. The mists were late in forming that morning, so that we were rewarded with glorious views of the west ridge and face, together with a great expanse of territory below us. The dark green of the forest merged into the wide grey-green sea of the plains, a vague, shadowy surface streaked with the darker lines of bush growing by the watercourses. This was bounded on the north by the Loldaika Hills, beyond which the green changed to brown, and the brown to yellow, as the arid sandy wastes which stretch to the Abyssinian Highlands took possession. To the south, cloud hid all but the loftiest of the Aberdares, allowing us no glimpse of the snows of Kilimanjaro, 200 miles away, which once or twice have been seen from high up on Kenya.

Our descent was enlivened by a variation which at first promised well, but later involved us in a long rappel; and on the way to camp we passed the skeleton of a buffalo at about 15,000 feet. We got home in a snowstorm at five o'clock, pretty tired.

In the night there were ten degrees of frost. We lay long in bed and had an easy day looking for a tarn which, from the top of Piggott, had attracted us by its brilliant, emerald-green colour.

West face of Mount Kenya, from Point Piggott, showing upper part of the west ridge on left

By permission of Alpine Journal

On the 8th we made a grand circular tour of the peak, passing to the west of Piggott, and by Two Tarn Col to the Lewis Glacier, which we crossed to get home again by four. Near Point Lenana we found a thermometer dropped by S.'s party in 1929; the height was about 16,000 feet and the minimum reading was thirteen degrees—nineteen degrees of frost. The extreme cold which we had felt, after our return from the traverse of the peak, even inside the hut, made us doubt the accuracy of this reading. We left a thermometer of our own in the same place to be collected later. The ponies were to come up for us on the 10th, so the 9th was devoted to the climbing of what we called Midget Peak, a very pointed and precipitous little rock needle on the south side of the mountain, which only lack of time had prevented us having a go at on the previous day. We fully expected the climbing of it would afford some amusement, nor were we disappointed.

We reached it by the same route at 9.30 a.m., and started climbing by a gully in which there was rather more snow and verglas on the rocks than we liked. Higher up the difficulties increased, progress became slow, and snow began falling steadily. I suppose we should have turned back, but mist hid the summit and we expected every pitch would prove to be the last. S. led over several critical steps, one of which, a sloping ice-ledge, I had later particular reason to remember.

A great block crowning the summit was reached soon after one o'clock. Mist hid everything, the snow fell more heavily, and we immediately began the descent, feeling some concern at the condition of the rocks, rendered doubly difficult now by the fresh snow. Crossing the sloping ledge with more haste than caution, the new snow came away and I with it. What happened then I do not know, for my next recollection is standing on a rock platform holding a disjointed conversation with S., who was now about eighty feet above me. My first question was true to form, because on the stage, when the heroine recovers from her faint, she usually gasps out, 'Where am I ?' before once more relapsing into semi-consciousness and the arms of her beloved. With me it was no idle question, because I had a very strong impression that we were on Kilimanjaro, an illusion only dispelled by repeated assurances to the contrary from S. Physically I seemed to be all right, but mentally I was all wrong—perhaps the jerk of the rope had knocked me senseless. Nor were my mental anxieties any less when I found that this descent of mine by a new and very quick route was of no use, because I had reached an impasse and had to climb back to join S., assisted by the rope.

A second attempt to traverse the iced-up ledge was successful, and the descent continued over rocks which seemed to become colder and more difficult every minute. Wherever it was possible, we roped down on a doubled rope, making eight or nine in all of these rappels. Had the descent continued much further we should have run out of rope, because we had to cut eighteen inches or more off each time to make a rope ring through which to pass the climbing-rope. We were singularly ill equipped for this travesty of climbing, necessary though it was, since we had with us not even a pocket-knife, so that the rope had to be hacked through with a sharp stone.

However, we got down, still with some rope in hand, collected the ice-axe and rucksack which we had left at the foot, and trudged heavily up the Lewis Glacier for the third time, in soft new snow. (This glacier, by the way, was named after a Professor Lewis, an American geologist who accomplished some revolutionary work in the study of glaciers.) It was not altogether a surprising thing that I now began to feel as though in the course of the day I had come into violent contact with something hard; in addition, both of us were very wet, and neither of us was strong-minded enough to deviate from our route to collect the thermometer left near Point Lenana. It was probably buried deep under snow anyway, and no doubt it still lies there, taking temperatures which no one will ever read.

On the 10th we did nothing but lament the fact that the ponies would not arrive until evening, for we now realised that we had very little food left to see us down. Three came up, and on the 11th we made a double march to our first camp at the edge of the forest, which was reached at five o'clock in rain. We had nothing left to eat but a small quantity of one of those food beverages which are a household word. Perhaps we had insufficient, but we began to suspect that the claims made for it were as hollow as our stomachs. This camp in the forest, which should have been doubly pleasant to our senses, starved by many days lived amongst rock and snow, was for us merely an irksome delay before the satisfying of our more animal wants.

We were horribly weak as we crawled feebly down next day to the farm from which we started. Bacon and eggs there at 10.30 a.m., and

Mount Kenya: The north face, showing the west ridge and Joseph Glacier
and (centre left) Point Peter

lunch and beer at noon, were partial restoratives, after which we set-tled our accounts, and left for home.

This was, I think, the most satisfying fortnight either of us ever spent or is ever likely to spend in Africa. On Kenya is to be found climbing at its best. There is no easy route up it, but much virtue may be got from a mountain without climbing it. For those who are not compelled to answer its challenge, let them camp near the solitudes of its glaciers, to gaze upon the fair face of the mountain in sunshine and shadow, to watch the ghostly mists writhing among the crags and pinnacles, and to draw strength from her ruggedness, repose from her aloofness.

Few are the countries that, having no traditions, have in their stead such a symbol and an inspiration.

CHAPTER V

BUSINESS AND PLEASURE

It [hunting] was the labour of the savages of North America,
but the amusement of the gentleman of England.
—SAMUEL JOHNSON

TWO OF AFRICA'S GREAT snow mountains had now been visited, and both had given to us great delight, but before we could round off our experiences on the third a hiatus of more than a year elapsed. For most of 1931 I was alone on the farm while S. was out of the country, but towards the end of the year I got away again, armed once more with a rifle instead of an ice-axe.

My excuse was an invitation from a friend, D., who occupied the next farm. 'Owned' the farm would be more correct, for he very seldom occupied it. Much of his time was spent on safari, for, like Nimrod, he was a mighty hunter to whom little came amiss but whose main preoccupation was elephant.

He had lately succeeded in following his favourite pursuit at someone else's expense by getting himself appointed a temporary Vermin Control Officer, or V.C.O., but this 'bureaucratese' requires some explanation. Like the A.D.C., who so interested the snobs of Handley Cross until they discovered that the letters implied a connection with drains and not with the Army, so, possibly, the municipal rat-catcher is referred to officially as the V.C.O. But the term vermin may include much more than rats or mice, for, just as weeds are a plant in the wrong place, so vermin are animals (of any kind) living where they are not wanted. In East Africa there are many such, and to the list of common vermin, animals such as elephants, buffalo, lions, rhinos, or zebra have from time to time to be added, should they become dangerous to the lives or injurious to the property of the natives. The calling of them vermin, which means that they can be shot without restrictions, is only temporary and local, and as soon as effective steps have been taken the usual shooting restrictions apply as before. These stipulate that only males can be shot, and limit the number of those which can be killed by the licence-holder in the year.

D.'s appointment was for the control (not the extinction) of a herd of about two thousand elephants. The herd's main stamping-ground was a valley (let us call it the Gubba) some thirty miles long, itself uninhabited, but situated in the middle of thickly populated country. The former dwellers in the Gubba had been driven out by the depredations of the herd, so that a large tract of fertile land had been lost to the native Reserve concerned. This was bad enough, but the herd might have been left in peace had it confined its wanderings to the valley instead of using it as a base from which to roam in all directions, moving to and from other feeding-grounds, doing enormous damage to the natives' crops *en route*.

A single elephant might easily destroy a quarter-acre plot of maize or bananas in a night, far more, of course, being trampled down than are actually eaten. The diameter of the foot of a full-grown bull is a good eighteen inches; the circumference, therefore, is nearly five feet, so that, allowing four of these meat plates to each, as we must, the devastation wrought by the passage of only a few of the two thousand can be imagined. The unfortunate natives, having no firearms, applied to the District Commissioner for protection, and D.'s appointment was the result. His orders were to drive the herd into some country on the other side of a big river thirty miles to the south-east—country occupied by a pastoral tribe who gave no hostages to fortune by growing crops. It was hoped that the elephants, with a little persuasion, would remain there, and one of the methods afterwards employed to effect this was more successful than seems likely. A wide and deep trench was dug for a length of about five miles on the near side of the river by their accustomed crossing-place, and it was not until a section of this fell in, through neglect on the part of the chief responsible for it, that the elephants began to find their way back.

This was the general idea; the tactics were left to D., whose plan was to harass them severely in and around the Gubba to get the main body moving, and kept moving, in the required direction. Like mankind, elephants follow their leaders and are creatures of habit, so this was not so difficult as it sounds; their appointed exile was also one of their familiar haunts, and in their forays from the valley they kept mostly to time-honoured paths. By shooting some of the more independent-minded, and by closing the paths with a dead elephant or two as a warning to others, D. hoped to confine them to beyond the river.

When I received his invitation to join him for a fortnight he had been at work on this for some months, and had moved all but about two hundred, which clung obstinately to their old haunts. In effecting it he had endured much, for the country is hot, wet, and unhealthy, while the harassing had not been all on one side. Thirty elephants had fallen in the campaign, and as time went on the survivors resented it more and more, and became increasingly cunning. The stubborn remnant comprised mainly immature bulls, and cows with calves at foot, who on that account were loth to travel and were less complaisant when hustled.

Provided with a shooting licence, a double-barrel .470, and a .256 rifle, I joined D., and we left for the Gubba in a battered Ford car buried under a mountainous load of kit. Very many decrepit bridges, not an inch wider than the wheel-track of the car, with nothing to keep the wheels on and every inducement wet and greasy mud could provide to make them slip off, were sufficient to occupy our minds for the drive of three hours. At the end of that time we stabled the car under a grass shelter and set about collecting porters to carry our stuff to D.'s old camp in the Gubba, on the other side of a ridge eight miles away.

This camp site was a charming one, perched high above the floor of the valley, sheltered amidst a clump of trees, and watered by a clear stream whose source was a spring near the top of the ridge. From the door of the tent we commanded several miles of the valley, while from a small spur half a mile away the field of view was even greater. The only drawback to an otherwise perfect situation was the waist-deep grass, concealing many boulders, whose presence made worse the cold, wet job of stumbling sleepily out of camp in the half-light of dawn, and increased the possibility of falls and damaged rifles.

The elephant kept to the valley bottom, which was only a mile across, and fairly open, except for a dense strip of bush on either side of the stream or series of muddy water-holes that lay in the middle of it. In places this strip almost filled the valley floor; at others it narrowed to a few yards; but it was nowhere penetrable except by following game tracks. It consisted largely of euphorbia-trees, which gave the bush a sinister aspect. Better known as the candelabra-tree, a name which well describes the shape, this is a dismal grey giant cactus. It is much disliked by the natives on account of the property the sap has (or is said to have) of blinding a man. The bushmen of South Africa use the juice of a euphorbia for poisoning their arrows.

Besides lesser game, the valley was the home of a herd of buffalo, and D. had seen tracks of rhino. Less tangible but more to be feared than these, were the tsetse fly, carrier of sleeping-sickness. The fly lives in thick bush, seems to require shade, and is never far from water. There are two principal species, *Glossina palpalis* and *Glossina morsitans*; the former is the carrier of sleeping-sickness while the other infects cattle with a fatal disease called 'fly.' It is now thought probable that their roles are interchangeable. For us the only way of avoiding this pest was to leave the bush before eight in the morning and not to enter it again until late in the evening.

While coming along in the car we had noticed recent tracks of elephant, and, after making camp, D. interviewed some local natives in order to bring his knowledge up to date—he had been away from the district for some weeks with a bad attack of fever. Meanwhile I took a light rifle and strolled along the hillside, where I saw some reedbuck and a herd of waterbuck. The reedbuck was Chandler's variety, which in spite of its name is never found near reeds but on stony hillsides. We wanted meat—or I have no doubt our porters did—but I did not shoot, because the locals reported that the buffalo herd was at this end of the valley and a shot might spoil our chances of bagging one. As a result of being shot at, elephant and buffalo are now the wariest of game, and the sound of a rifle, even at a distance, is enough to make them leave the locality. For this reason there is much to be said in favour of a light rifle, the report of which does not disturb a whole district as does the roar of a big double-barrel rifle.

Next morning D., who was still convalescent, stayed in camp, when I turned out at five, again carrying only a light rifle, to wander slowly up the valley skirting the edge of the bush. I was very much on the *qui vive*. According to the natives, an elephant which D. had wounded was still hereabouts. I saw nothing until at seven o'clock, as I was about to turn for home and breakfast, out of the corner of one eye I caught a glimpse of what looked like the tail of an elephant disappear into the bush. The wounded elephant had been looming large in my imagination—an imagination quickened by a lack of food—to the exclusion of all else. I had only the little .256 rifle, so instead of closer investigation I returned at once to camp for a heavier weapon. On the way I shot two kongoni for our meat-hungry porters. Having seen nothing of the buffalo or their spoor, I concluded the natives had been mistaken when they told us the buffalo were in this part of the valley.

After some food D. accompanied me back to the scene of my ignominious flight. He was a bit sceptical, and rather thought I had been seeing things, and now I was not so sure myself, for my glimpse had been but a fleeting one, and of only a tail at that. It was therefore a surprise for both of us when we found from the spoor that the tail I saw was not an imaginary one, and that it belonged, not to an elephant, but to a buffalo.

It was then too late in the day to do anything, because the buffalo would be lying up in the bush. I kicked myself for having missed such a chance, and no doubt D. wanted to kick me too for my unwary shots at the kongoni. However, even if the buffalo were alarmed they would not stir before evening; we were therefore back again at sunset. Our perseverance was rewarded by a hurried snapshot which D. took, and missed, at a big bull running across a grass glade. That was all we saw.

Next morning we were out again from five to nine to find the herd had moved down the valley, whither, in the evening, we followed them—but they had gone too far.

This bare recital illustrates the difficulty of getting a shot at wary game even though their whereabouts are more or less known. We knew where they were, had devoted two days to them, and had had only one very slim chance; all very dull, possibly, to read about, but great fun in the doing. The pursuit was full of interest—indeed, excitement, since in this type of country you can never tell what you may not meet round the corner.

Meanwhile our native intelligence department had definitely located the elephant in a stretch of very bad bush some ten miles down the valley, towards which we now moved camp. It had rained hard every night since our arrival, and we had barely packed the sodden tents before it started again. It was a wet, warm, and exhausting march, mainly because the floor of the valley was compounded of black cotton soil, of which vile, sticky stuff our boots picked up several pounds at each step. Camp was not reached until afternoon.

The valley here was much wider, so that to be within striking distance of the bush we had to camp in a far less pleasing spot almost in the bottom, where mosquitoes were troublesome. A side valley, the Aru, came in close to the camp, and we were about two miles from where we expected to find the elephant.

That evening we went down to the bush but found no spoor, and on the way home D. was tempted by a roan antelope with a very good head. The wind was setting away from the bush, nor had we seen any sign of the elephant, so he risked disturbing them and loosed off. After a stern chase and a second shot the big roan was brought to bag, and we got back to camp long after dark with the head.

Three days had thus passed without any hostilities in the warfare against the elephant, but this morning we were to have an affair of outposts. Down in the bush by six, we soon came on fresh spoor, and a little later heard elephants trumpeting. For an hour we manoeuvred in dense bush, trying hard to keep a chancy wind right and to get a sight of something. The tension increased every minute. We were all keyed up, and had almost had enough, when, suddenly, thanks mainly to a very good Lumbwa tracker of D.'s, we found ourselves regarding a solitary bull elephant standing in a little clearing twenty yards away, offering an easy shot. He had very poor teeth, but that did not matter. D. promptly fired both barrels, but failed to drop him, and then followed a most startling conjuring trick. The elephant vanished instantaneously into the bush with a fearsome crash, and in his place stood a rhino, weaving his head to and fro in a puzzled but threatening manner.

It must have been immediately behind the elephant, and it was very strange that these two great beasts should have consorted together in this manner. I was told by D. of a case where the body of a rhino he had shot had been moved a distance of 200 yards by some elephants. It is not uncommon to see herds of antelope mixed up with kongoni, wildebeeste, and eland, grazing happily together, but in their case it is probable that other animals like to be near the kongoni, which are of a particularly alert and watchful nature, in order to have timely notice of the approach of any danger.

We stood facing each other for a matter of minutes until the rhino showed signs of wishing to investigate the cause of the disturbance, upon which D. fired again. He, too, disappeared with a crash little less loud than that of his companion, leaving us there in the thickest of bush with a wounded elephant and a wounded rhino on our hands, and the rest of the elephant herd all round us.

With infinite caution we slowly followed the rhino spoor through dangerously thick stuff for a hundred yards. The sound of a long-drawn breath stopped us as if shot, but the bush was so dense that some minutes passed before we could make out the form of a rhino facing us, not ten yards away. D. fired, stepping hastily back as he did so. The rhino fell and got up again, but, taking D.'s place, I finished it off.

The removal of one possible source of unpleasantness made us feel slightly easier. We advanced to examine the rhino, and were at once struck by the fact that the horn now seemed much smaller than that which had menaced us in the first place, which we had remarked as a particularly fine specimen. A cry from the tracker made us both jump, for we were still rather on edge, but, looking round, we saw him pointing, and there, a few yards from him, lay the body of another rhino. There were two, and this was the elephant's companion whose last breath it was we had heard.

It was an unfortunate affair, because we had no wish to kill a rhino, much less two, but from the time of firing at the elephant no other course was open to us, and, considering all other things, we were well out of it. Having taped the long horn, which measured thirty-one inches, we decided to get out of the bush and leave the wounded elephant till next day. The tsetse fly were becoming active, and we had had a busy morning and no breakfast.

The shortest way home led through a long stretch of bush, through which we passed with some apprehension by means of game trails. Much spoor indicated the presence of the whole herd, and D. knew from experience that when alarmed they could remain uncannily and deceptively quiet. It was eerie work in the gloom of the euphorbias, and when an elephant passed like a wraith not thirty yards from us, we froze instinctively in our tracks. He was moving fast and quite noiselessly. All we saw was a momentary glimpse of his ribs. As he passed behind us he got our wind, whereupon there was one loud crash as he changed direction, and then silence. The fright was mutual.

We returned to the scene at dawn next day with some porters to chop out the horns, and, having started them on this, we took up the spoor of the elephant.

The porters did not relish being left alone with the dead rhinos; even the thought of five tons of meat failed to cheer them. They imagined the surrounding bush to be alive with elephants, and, admittedly, this time they had more grounds for their fears than was usual. True, the elephants were no longer there, but twenty-four hours ago they had been, and to a native this was almost the same thing and quite sufficient cause for alarm. These particular natives, of an agricultural and not very intelligent tribe of Nilotic negroes, had an ingrained fear of the bush. Even if they could be persuaded to enter it, they were quite useless at finding their way about or moving quietly. On the other hand, D.'s tracker, who was a Lumbwa, was perfectly at home in it, and coolness itself when there was dangerous game about. We could always rely on him for that extra pair of keen eyes and sensitive ears which are so essential for hunting of this kind.

There was one exception amongst the porters: a man whom D. had told off to accompany me. He was an oldish man, not much use as a tracker, a complete clown, the butt of the camp, and apparently insensible to fear. He seemed to cherish a private grudge against all large game, and was never happier than when in pursuit of them. Carrying a light spear, he would barge about, quite unconcerned, in horrible proximity to elephant and buffalo; and to less ardent fire-eaters like myself seemed inconveniently eager to come to close action in the shortest possible time.

To return to the chase; our hopes were soon dashed. We could find no blood spoor, and the tracks soon became inextricably mingled with those of the herd, which had apparently left the bush and gone up to the Aru Valley during the night. They must have passed close to the camp. This wounded elephant was subsequently found dead by some natives not far from where he was hit.

In the afternoon we went up a hill overlooking the Aru Valley. The bush was less dense here, and towards evening we spotted the great black backs of the buffalo grazing slowly up. The herd kept inside the bush, but presently two glorious bulls moved out into a glade. This was not what we were there for, but I at any rate was not on duty and the chance was too good to miss. As a guest, I was to take the first shot, and after a long and very careful stalk we got within seventy yards of the biggest bull. Unluckily, when the time came to shoot I was behind D., and it was too late to change places, for the bull was already suspicious. Had we been sure of the wind and the buffalo we might have bandied politenesses like the Gentlemen of the Guard at Fontenoy, but, as it was, D. rightly took his chance and dropped the bull with a shot in the chest. The herd stampeded in a flash and no second chance offered.

The horns were a fine pair, old and gnarled, and over thirty-six inches long. Not content with that, D. also wanted the skin, which is highly prized by the natives, who will gladly give a heifer in exchange for one. They like buffalo hide for making their shields. Only the Lumbwa and the Clown were with us, but the shot soon drew a horde of men, women, and children, carrying baskets in anticipation of free meat. In spite of this willing assistance, it was dark before the long job of skinning was finished, and when the crowd understood that the skin had to be carried back to camp that night they melted away as a crowd does at the announcement of a silver collection. The skin was very big, a good inch thick over the shoulders, and, of course, wet, so the weight was enormous. In addition, it had to be carried over two miles of rough going—to our porters a disagreeable thought, but not so disagreeable as the idea of leaving the remnants of the carcase to others—humans or hyenas.

D.'s determination, backed by a forcible manner, prevailed, so that soon a gang of ten were staggering along under a strong sapling round which the skin was draped. We had to stay with them every step of the way or the precious hide would have been thrown to the hyenas forthwith. We rested when they rested, which was often, and it was two hours later before the party, now almost mutinous, arrived in camp. However, they had contrived to bring some meat as well as the skin, and when this was sizzling over the fire they ceased reviling the oppressor and began blessing their benefactor.

The following morning D. attended to cleaning the trophies while I walked over to a distant hill across the valley, known to D. as Lion

Hill. A month back he had come across eleven lions near this hill, but very wisely left them alone. No such sight rewarded me for a long, hot walk, and when I got back to camp I was disgusted to find D. had gone up the Aru on fresh news of the elephant. But I missed nothing. He had not been able to get near them, but had loosed off a few rounds to keep them on the move. This was effective, for the next day we learnt that they had retreated up the Gubba again, whither we must now follow.

So ended the first round with honours easy, or perhaps slightly in our favour, for the elephants were on the run and badly frightened. Regarded merely as a shooting trip it had been more than successful, but D. in his capacity of V.C.O. would have to be discreet about that side of the business, and we hoped that the next round would make up for any remissness on our part, as indeed it did.

CHAPTER VI

BUSINESS AND PLEASURE

—————◆—————

And o'er unhabitable downs,
Place elephants for want of towns.

—SWIFT

W E WERE GLAD TO EXCHANGE the heat and smells of the valley
camp for the cool freshness of our old eyrie on the hillside; the
porters' larder, which was now overstocked with rhino and buffalo
meat, was an offence in the eyes of heaven if not in those of our men. A
native never throws anything away or leaves anything behind; old tins,
old bottles, old clothes, and old meat—especially old meat—are their
delight, so that, as a safari proceeds, and one fondly imagines the loads
to be getting lighter, the reverse is the case. All the old rubbish which
has long since been thankfully discarded will be found, if one troubles
to look, packed carefully away in the loads as treasured possessions,
and, in addition, there will be samples of meat and bits of skin, in every
stage of decay, from all the animals that have been shot since the safari
started.

The morning after our return we sat on Observatory Hill, as we
had named the little spur close to the camp, raking the valley bottom
with our glasses. We sat there till nearly eight o'clock, and just as we
were about to give up D. spotted five cows moving up the valley. We
dashed down in hot haste, but by the time we had picked up their
spoor they had already retired to the thickest cover against the heat of
the day.

The evening was another blank. Nothing was moving, and we concluded that the main herd were now past our camp and near the head
of the valley, probably on the way out.

After nearly a year's experience of his herd, D. and his tracker
knew their habits and the country in which they moved like a book,
and could predict with uncanny certainty their probable movements.

Our next attempt to come to grips was based on this knowledge, and was very nearly successful.

Ten miles up, the valley narrowed to a neck through which the herd must pass on the way out. Here the hills came down steeply on each side, and between them was less than a quarter of a mile of short grass and thorn-trees. Above and below the neck was the abominable bush in which it was so difficult to move or see, but if we could only catch them crossing the open ground in daylight we could probably kill three or four and frighten the others out of the Gubba for good.

Such was our plan, but now a boy brought news that some of the elephant D. had already driven out were beginning to come back across the river. This called for prompt action, and meant that we could not stay here much longer but must get away to the river to stop them from filtering back to rejoin the small herd of 'die-hards' which had been leading us such a dance.

The upshot was that next morning we returned to the car, and sent the porters on with the main camp to a known camp site by the river. We ourselves, the Lumbwa tracker, and the Clown, with a light camp, made a long detour by car to a place as near to the neck as we could approach. We got there by midday, parked our bus under a shady thorn-tree, and walked over to the neck some two miles away. We were pleased to find by the absence of spoor that the elephant had not yet passed, and we sat there expectantly until dark, but nothing came. Talking things over that night under our tree, D. took a gloomy view of our chances, because the odds were heavily in favour of their coming through in the night.

We were up at four and on the ground by five, only to find our fears realised. The herd had passed in the night and was now probably in the sanctuary of the bush. We followed hot-foot, hoping to come up with them feeding near the edge. But it was too late; there was not a sound, and we saw nothing.

Afterwards we found that at one point the herd must have been just inside the bush when we passed outside quite unsuspectingly. Such a thing was disconcerting, not to say alarming, for normally a feeding herd can be readily detected by the crash of breaking branches, the squealing, and the noise of stomach-rumbling. Here we had passed within a few yards of them without being aware of it, so that if they had got our wind a sudden charge by some angry cow would have caught us off our guard.

They had beaten us again, but as a last gambler's throw we arranged that I should return to the neck and that D. would fire some random shots in the hope of frightening them back towards me. This was done, and D. told me afterwards that they had got into a fine state of panic, but it was too late in the day to expect them to leave the shade of the bush and nothing broke in my direction.

While waiting there for something to happen I heard first a single shot and then the sounds as of a brisk battle from D.'s heavy rifle, and though I was eager, like Napoleon's well-drilled marshals, to march to the sound of the guns, I dared not leave the neck unguarded. At ten o'clock I gave it up and returned to the car, where I learnt from D. that he had enjoyed a more interesting morning than I had. After his first shot to get the elephant moving he had actually seen one, and fired some ineffective shots at long range; on the way home he had tried for an impala, that most graceful of antelopes, and also had two snap shots at a leopard. What a thoroughly mixed bag it would have been if he had got all three.

The scene now shifts to the river for the last act, to that part of it near the elephants' crossing-place on which all their routes converge. Like most African rivers, there was on both banks a narrow strip of dense bush, but outside this the country was more open. It was hilly and broken, covered with short grass and scattered thorn-trees, allowing a range of visibility of a good hundred yards—on the whole much easier country for our purpose than the Gubba.

It is a common mistake to camp too near to the intended hunting-ground. Our camp, therefore, was pitched two miles from the river, but, even so, the elephant down by the ford were noisy enough during the night to be heard by us—perhaps they had got our wind even at that distance. The scent and hearing of an elephant are most acute. One very experienced elephant hunter considers that they can scent a man at a greater range than any other animal—perhaps at 600 yards or more—but that they cannot sight anything at more than fifty yards, even though it is on the skyline.

Next morning we made a long round, heard one scream, but saw nothing; while from two o'clock till seven we were out again further up the river. Coming home we again heard one, when we ran for a couple of miles, but failed to come up with them.

For several days now I had been having trouble with a knee that had gone completely stiff so that I had to walk with one leg a 'swinger.' This 'dot and carry one' was a painful business, and, plodding home after this exhausting day, I tried to convince D. of what was now crystal clear to me, that to camp two miles from our scene of action was carrying caution to absurd lengths.

'Two b— miles of b— absurdity' was the text on which I preached. It made no impression on D., who had not got a dud leg, but I forgave him because he had an excellent theory, which, moreover, he carried into practice, that in order to keep fit on safari you must do yourself rather better than when at home. The bottles which exemplified this theory travelled in company with a syphon in a specially constructed four-gallon petrol tin with a hinged lid, and when this was under the table between us we soon forgot tired legs, stiff joints, and elephants that behaved like will-o'-the-wisps.

In the old days in South Africa, before fear of man drove them into thick bush and forest, the elephants were hunted on ponies; a pony that was staunch in the presence of elephant, and would allow one of the old elephant-guns (a young cannon like a 4-bore) to be fired from off its back, was a thing of great value. Nowadays a stout pair of legs are more useful. It was, I think, the celebrated hunter Stigand, whose opinion of the scenting powers of elephant I have just quoted, who reckoned that, failures included, every elephant killed had cost him one hundred miles of walking.

We repeated the round next morning, and yet once more in the afternoon. Towards evening we climbed a hill overlooking the ford and sat there listening to the very noisy mob down below in the bush. Suddenly, from directly behind us, came one shrill, solitary trumpet. Our chance had come.

Heading away from the bush, we had not far to go before we located about a dozen elephants, mostly cows and young bulls, in fairly easy country. Cows are, of course, protected in the ordinary way, but for our purpose a dead cow was as effective as a dead bull.

Taking advantage of their short range of vision, and troubling only to keep the wind right, we got to within fifty yards before being seen. The biggest of the cows then swung round to face us, ears stuck out and trunk erect, looking indeed 'wiciously wenomous,' as John Jorrocks would have said. D. fired, and she came for us at the shot. I fired and turned her, and D., taking advantage of the broadside presented as she swerved, poured in more lead. He was taking no chances. Meanwhile I succeeded in dropping two more, and D. one, before the rest broke for the river, where we hoped that their panic might infect the others and carry the whole lot over.

D. thought that these may have been some of our friends from the Gubba in search of a quieter neighbourhood, or possibly forerunners of the main body. The ivory was all small, but it was then too late to cut it out, so we returned for it early next day. On the way down we were disappointed to hear a pandemonium still raging at the river; it was evident there was an agitated discussion in progress, but what the upshot would be we could not tell.

Before leaving camp we had given the word to pack. My leave was at an end and D. was willing to give the elephant a breathing-space so that this last lesson might sink in. He had also a chance now of fulfilling a commission given him by some learned body in England engaged in research work, which was to obtain for them the foetus of an elephant.

Neither of us knew the first thing about an elephant's interior arrangements, nor had we gone closely into the means of preservation and despatch beyond providing ourselves with a five-gallon drum of methylated spirits. This drum we had solemnly carted about with us from camp to camp, much to the chagrin of the porter who had to carry it. Our men were curious as to the contents, and from the way we cherished it thought it must be some potent spirit, as indeed it was: but had we explained the base uses to which it was to be put they would have been more than ever convinced of our madness. This drum was about twelve inches in diameter and eighteen inches deep, and our plan, beautiful in its simplicity, was merely to remove the lip, drop in our specimen, and solder it up.

However, there was now no time to waste; the cows had been dead for twelve hours and we set about our grisly task. In one of them we found what we wanted, and, having imbued the boys with some of our recently kindled enthusiasm for science, they extracted it with the greatest care. When at last it was laid at our feet for inspection, we found it measured about four feet by two and weighed every bit of two hundred pounds. Our five-gallon drum, which was standing open-mouthed in readiness, looked rather foolish—our own mouths must have stood open in sympathy. The problem of getting a quart into a pint pot seemed, in comparison, simple, but D. was not to be beaten by a trifle like that, and bethought him of a forty-gallon oil-drum now lying empty on his farm seventy miles away. He forthwith decided we must go there, quickly, specimen and all. The mild objections to having the repulsive mass lying at our feet as a fellow-traveller for that distance, which I raised, were brushed contemptuously aside.

By now it was nine o'clock, and getting warm. Already the air bore to the sensitive nostril something more than a hint that speed was essential if our gift was to be at all acceptable to science. A stretcher of branches was rigged up, and six of our stoutest porters hoisted the whole thing on to their shoulders. Grass and leaves were then strewn over it to protect it from the sun and to keep off the flies, and the cortege started at a most unfuneral pace for the car. In spite of frequent relays of porters we did not get there until midday, but camp had already been struck and everything was ready.

The elephant in embryo was slid gently from the stretcher into the box-body of the car, which it almost filled, while to avoid doing it any damage our kit was festooned round the bonnet and the wings. D. took the wheel and off we sped over a shockingly bad road. After an hour D. succumbed to an attack of fever, so that I had to take over the driving. I am never fond of driving a car with the critical owner of it sitting beside me as a passenger, and now everything conspired to make the position an unenviable one. Neither of us was feeling very amiable. It was a disgustingly hot day, our kit kept dropping off, and the other passenger at the back was beginning to make its presence felt. The luckless driver could do nothing right; if I hit the innumerable ruts and pot-holes too hard I was accused of lack of skill or deliberately attempting to break up the car; if, on the other hand, I drove too carefully, I was rated for allowing our unique specimen to go bad on our hands, thus showing a pitiful lack of enthusiasm for the great cause of scientific research in which we were now enlisted as humble but active pioneers; moreover, it was pointed out that if such a fate did overtake our precious burden, our names, mine particularly, would stink for ever in the nostrils of biologists with a stink far worse than that from which we were now shrinking.

At four o'clock, when we were about half-way, we reached an Administrative Post, where there was a hospital for natives, the doctor of which was a friend of D.'s. We stopped for advice, thinking, not unnaturally, that here was something after their own hearts. The experts there were interested but pessimistic. Accustomed only to seeing paltry specimens tucked comfortably away in little glass bottles, the Brobdingnagian scale of ours seemed to deprive them of any imagination or inventive resource they may have had. They talked learnedly but vaguely of formalin injections, but were unable to say off-hand how many pints or gallons would be needed, and at length hinted broadly that they had neither formalin nor time to waste. Meanwhile the passenger at the back, for whose benefit we had stopped, complained loudly of the delay, so, thanking them, but with our faith in the usefulness of doctors shaken, we drove on desperately. It was 'night or Blücher,' the oil-drum or the grave.

We got in without further adventure about dark, and called urgently for boys and lights to assist at the obsequies or the pickling. The Thing had stood the journey fairly well, but looked a bit wan in the light of the lanterns. A friend who was present had the hardihood to suggest that it had been hung a shade too long—a piece of facetiousness that struck me as dangerous in view of D.'s choleric mood.

It was ticklish work getting it into the drum, with D. hopping about and cursing everybody in his anxiety lest at the last moment his flawless specimen should receive some irreparable injury. To say it was poured in would be an exaggeration—insinuated, perhaps, describes it better; but, anyhow, in it went, and now all depended upon our precious five gallons of methylated spirits.

The suspense was frightful, as this was swallowed in the cavernous depths of the big drum, and agonising were our doubts as to whether the spirit would be sufficient to cover everything. Happily it sufficed, and with a last affectionate glance at the dreadful Thing inside we popped the lid on and sealed it up. We went to dinner, proud of the day's work and our unique specimen, with our appetites unimpaired by memories of its recent past or fears for its future.

I left next day, and that was the last I saw of D. and the oil-drum for some time. I often wondered how it had fared on the long journey of seventy miles to the station, 500 miles in the fierce heat of a steel truck to the coast, and yet fiercer heat of the Red Sea; and even more did I wonder what the biological consignee thought of it. The true story is shrouded in mystery, and I fear it will never be revealed. Perhaps the drum was never delivered, because, shortly after, I read in a paper of a truck on the Uganda Railway being derailed by the explosion of an oil-drum. I had an uneasy feeling that there might have been some connection.

Later I heard that D. had controlled his vermin so well that his services were no longer needed and he lost his job. All had been rounded up and banished to beyond the river except for a remnant of 'die-hards' which still clung stubbornly to the Gubba. I believe he even found a solution to another problem in practical biology, but it was probably one of less formidable dimensions than ours.

CHAPTER VII

RUWENZORI:
THE MOUNTAINS OF THE MOON

And with Caesar to take in his hand
the army, the empire, and Cleopatra,
and say, 'All these will I relinquish if
you will show me the fountain of the Nile.'

—EMERSON

THE RIFLES WERE OILED and packed away, and, after the rather forced gaieties of an African Christmas, I took the ice-axe from its corner preparatory to joining S. on his farm. We had in mind a journey to Ruwenzori in January of 1932, that month being specially picked because in most parts of East Africa it is the driest. This forethought went unrewarded.

The Ruwenzori range seems to me to combine the greatest geographical and historical interest of any part of Africa; true, historically, Egypt must take pride of place, but somehow I have never been able to regard Egypt as part of Africa; it seems more akin to Asia, though it is so inseparably connected with the Nile, a connection that is expressed in the aphorism: 'The Nile is Egypt and Egypt is the Nile.' These Ruwenzori mountains are the birthplace of the Nile, the Fons Nilus of the ancients, and their existence was for more than 2000 years a field for discussion, speculation, and endeavour by Egyptian, Greek, Roman, Hindu, Arab, and European. The discovery by Stanley in 1888 of this range of mountains whose snows feed the two lakes from which the greatest of the Nile branches takes its source, brought to an end the long quest for the sources of this classic river.

The first hint we have that their existence was known in very early times is a verse in Æschylus which speaks of 'Egypt nurtured by snow,' and Aristotle in the fourth century B.C. mentions the 'Mountains of

Silver, the source of the Nile.' The Greeks themselves were active in trade and exploration on the Upper Nile and round the East African coast, but they were probably only followers in the footsteps of Arabs, Phoenicians, Egyptians, or even Hindus. Speke, when preparing for his journey which culminated in his discovery of the Ripon Falls, where the Nile leaves Victoria Nyanza, secured his best information from the Hindu sacred books, the Puranas: 'All our previous information,' he says, 'concerning the hydrography of these regions originated with the ancient Hindus, who told it to the priests of the Nile; and all those busy Egyptian geographers... in solving the mystery which enshrouded the source of their holy river were so many hypothetical humbugs. The Hindu traders had a firmer basis to stand upon, through their intercourse with the Abyssinians.' The Puranas trace the course of the Nile to a great lake, mention Zanzibar, Lake Tanganyika, the Karagwe Mountains (in Uganda), and Unyamwezi, the Country of the Moon.

Under the settled rule of the Roman Empire the Greek merchants in Egypt prospered, and we read of one of them, Diogenes, who, returning from a voyage to India, landed on the east coast at Rhaptum (Pangani, near Tanga); thence he claimed to have travelled inland for a journey of twenty-five days until he arrived in the vicinity of 'two great lakes and the snowy range of mountains whence the Nile draws its twin sources.' He was told that the Nile united its head streams at a point north of the great lakes, whence it flowed through marshes to the Blue Nile and so to Egypt. The time taken—twenty-five days—rather invalidates his story of having seen the snow mountains unless it was Kilimanjaro or Kenya that he saw (and there, of course, there is no lake), but the information he brought back, from whatever source derived, was amazingly accurate, and was evidently based on something more than guesswork. The story is told by Ptolemy, the great Greek geographer writing about A.D. 150, and he it is who has received the credit for the theory of the origin of the Nile, which was not proved until seventeen centuries later.

It is from him that we get the name Mountains of the Moon, for on his map he called the Karagwe Mountains 'Lunae Montis finis occidentalis,' and, for the confusion of subsequent explorers and geographers, Kilimanjaro is shown as Lunæ Montis finis orientalis. This

Ruwenzori: Mount Stanley, photographed from the air

classical tradition that 'the sources of the Nile were to be found in two lakes whose waters were fed by the snow melting on the Mountains of the Moon, south of the equator,' was handed down unchallenged. Mediæval maps and descriptions, Arab and European, reproduce the Mountains of the Moon and the equatorial lakes with various probable and improbable modifications in spite of a complete lack of any confirmation of their existence.

When Krapf and Rebmann discovered the mountains of Kilimanjaro and Kenya in 1848, it was at once thought that these were Ptolemy's Mountains of the Moon, although there is no lake near either of them, nor are they in any way connected with the Nile basin.

In 1861 Speke discovered the Mfumbiro volcanoes, a group of volcanic peaks 12,000 feet to 14,000 feet high lying between Lakes Kivu and Albert Edward, and claimed that these were the Mountains of the Moon. He was on surer ground, because a tributary of the Kagera River, one of the most remote sources of the Victoria Nile, rises here, but there is a fatal objection in that there is no snow on any of these peaks, which thus fail to answer Ptolemy's description.

In the twenty years preceding Stanley's discovery of Ruwenzori in 1888, many explorers had traversed the same country and sailed upon the waters of Victoria, but none had suspected the near presence of this region of snow and ice, hidden as it was in the clouds and vapours which are a persistent and dominating feature of the range. Indeed, in 1875, when circumnavigating Victoria, Stanley himself was camped on the eastern slopes and relates, without comment, the assertions of the natives that above him there were mountains of extraordinary size and of a shining whiteness; and it was only on a later journey, in 1888, that he was vouchsafed the almost incredible vision of these snow mountains, practically on the equator, which by then had become almost fabulous. 'While looking to the southeast and meditating upon the events of the last month, my eyes were attracted by a boy to a mountain, said to be covered with salt, and I saw a peculiar-shaped cloud of a most beautiful silver colour which assumed the proportions and appearance of a vast mountain covered with snow. Following its form downwards, I became struck with the deep blue-black colour of its base, and wondered if it portended another tornado; then, as the sight descended to the gap between the eastern and western plateaux, I became for the

first time conscious that what I gazed upon was not the image or sem-
blance of a vast mountain, but the solid substance of a real one, its
summit covered with snow.'

To these mountains Stanley gave the name Ruwenzori, as being
that by which they were most widely known amongst the natives of
the surrounding regions. It was, naturally, only an approximation to
the sound they uttered when questioned by Stanley on the subject.
Amongst the natives whom we employed on the mountain, the word,
or our way of uttering it, had no meaning whatsoever. This is only to
be expected, because the numerous tribes who live near the mountains
probably have, and in those days certainly had, very little intercourse.
Even those living on the same side of the range have different lan-
guages and mix very little, while those on opposite sides might as well
be in different worlds for all they know or see of each other. Nor would
any native think of giving a name to the whole range, but would only
name, if at all, some particular peak which might be prominently seen
from his village.

Stanley attributed the obscurity, in which the mountains seemed
to be always wrapped by cloud, to vapours exhaled from the surrounding plains saturated by rain and then exposed to the fierce heat of an
equatorial sun. The rainfall to the east of the range is about sixty inches
annually; on the west it is heavier; while on the northern slopes it is
said to reach 200 inches.

Stanley's opinion that Ptolemy's Mountains of the Moon had at last
been identified did not go unchallenged. Some learned pundits maintained that Kenya and Kilimanjaro were the mountains in question,
and, as has been seen, Ptolemy did call the last-named Lunae Montis
finis orientalis, presumably in the belief that a great range stretched for
five hundred miles from Ruwenzori in the west to Kilimanjaro in the
east. But neither Kilimanjaro nor Kenya is remotely connected with the
Nile basin, and the only argument in support of this contention is that
these two mountains are far more likely to have been seen by very early
travellers than the inaccessible Ruwenzori range.

Others identified the Mountains of the Moon with the Mfumbiro
volcanoes, in accordance with Speke's notion, and yet others accepted
the explanation advanced by the German explorer, Dr O. Baumann.
He discovered that one source of the Kagera, mentioned above as the

main tributary of the Victoria Nile, was situated in the mountains of Missosi ya Mwesi, north-east of Lake Tanganyika. This name does in fact mean the 'Mountains of the Moon,' the surrounding country is known as Charo cha Mwesi, or the Lands of the Moon, and the people of it are Mwana ya Mwesi, the People of the Moon. That this romantic title should actually be applied to the mountains of this country by the natives was at least a strange coincidence, but their insignificant altitude and comparative unimportance incline one to the belief that it was nothing more, or, perhaps, the mistaken transference of the name by ancient geographers to mountains more worthy of it.

The mountains of Abyssinia are also competitors for the title and are not without their backers, but to the plain man it seems clear enough that the only mountains answering in all respects to Ptolemy's description are those which we now call Ruwenzori. To argue otherwise appeals strongly to the upholders of lost causes, of whom there is never any lack, and no doubt to the end of time people will be found maintaining stoutly that Bacon wrote Shakespeare's plays, that the earth is flat, or that the Ruwenzori Mountains are not Ptolemy's Mountains of the Moon. But it is time to leave this interesting but profitless speculation and to recount briefly the history of the more recent exploration of Ruwenzori, wherein ascertainable facts take the place of cloudy theory.

The first to penetrate the mountains was Stanley's assistant, Lieutenant W. G. Stairs. He approached from the west, and reached an altitude of about 10,000 feet. In 1891 Dr F. Stuhlmann made a five-day excursion up one of the western valleys, attaining a point not far below the snow-line which he estimated to be 13,300 feet. He it was who recognised that Ruwenzori was not a single mountain, but a range, and who accurately described the successive zones of vegetation from foothills to snow-line. Four years later G. F. Scott Elliott, a naturalist, made several journeys from the west, and was the first to find a route from the east up the Mobuku Valley, by which route all subsequent successes were achieved, save that of a Belgian expedition, which climbed the peaks from the western side in 1932.

The closing years of the last century were years of stress and turmoil for Uganda, for it was at that time gradually being brought under British administration. The country was in a very disturbed state, and no more exploration was done around Ruwenzori until 1900, when

C. S. Moore ascended the Mobuku Valley to a height of 14,900 feet and was the first to reach the glaciers lying at its head. He confirmed Stuhlmann's observations, which distributed the peaks amongst four main groups. Three other parties, including that of Sir Harry Johnston, the exceedingly versatile High Commissioner of the Uganda Protectorate, followed him in the same year, and another a year later, so the route was becoming well known.

Transport problems, too, were very much simpler than formerly. In 1902 the Uganda Railway was opened to the east side of Lake Victoria, and steamers ran from railhead to Entebbe, the capital of Uganda on the north-west shore of the Lake, only 200 miles from Fort Portal, at the north end of the range. Moreover, with the crushing of the insurrection of 1897, the country was rapidly pacified, and travellers could move about with some sense of security.

In November 1905 the mountains were attacked for the first time by a party of mountaineers, but on this occasion the weather proved to be a sufficient defence. Douglas Freshfield, A. L. Mumm, with the guide Moritz Inderbinnen, reached the head of the Mobuku Valley, but were prevented by persistent rain from doing more than reach the snows. Early in the following year a party sent out by the British Museum to study the flora and fauna of Ruwenzori spent several weeks in the Mobuku Valley. A. F. Wollaston (an experienced mountaineer and explorer) and H. B. Woosnam climbed a small peak on the ridge west of the valley, and so reached a height of over 16,000 feet.

It was left to the Italians to achieve not only the first success, but a success so sweeping that little was left to be done afterwards, and mountaineering expeditions of the same nationality have upheld the reputation then gained for thoroughness of organisation on the mountains of Alaska and in the Himalaya. From what has been said it will be clear that, when the Duke of Abruzzi took his large and well-equipped expedition out in the summer of 1906, little was known of the mountains except the best line of access; the position, number, and height of the snow peaks were only guessed at, estimates of the last ranging from 16,000 feet to 18,000 feet.

Apart from climbing the highest peaks, the objects of the expedition included a survey of the range and the study of geology, glaciology, botany, zoology, and meteorology. To carry out this ambitious programme there were twelve Europeans, including six scientists, four guides, a photographer, and a cook. The magnitude of the undertaking and the skill required to organise it can be gathered from the fact that over 300 porters were employed—a generous figure, but modest when compared with the numbers of some recent Himalayan expeditions— German, French, Italian, and British. Experience rather suggests that the success of an expedition is in inverse ratio to its magnitude, but to this the Duke of the Abruzzi's party was a marked exception. A dozen snow peaks, including Margherita, 16,815 feet; and Alexandra, 16,749 feet, the two highest, were climbed for the first time, while on some the ascent was repeated several times for purposes of survey. An accurate map of the peaks, glaciers, and high valleys was made, a mass of meteorological and other observations collected, and a wealth of botanical, zoological, and geological information gathered and speci- mens brought back. That all this work should have been accomplished in the course of six weeks is the more remarkable when the handicap of 'Ruwenzori weather' is taken into account. Perhaps this expedition was more favoured by the weather than most, but from their records it appears that there were few days when the peaks remained clear after eight in the morning, while for the whole of June and the first week in July bad weather predominated. The only fine spell was in the second week in July, when the retreat from the higher valleys had already begun.

It was twenty years later before the highest peaks of Ruwenzori were again climbed, this time by an English party led by Dr Noel Humphreys. In these two successful expeditions the extremes of size almost meet. Dr Humphreys was accompanied by one other European and perhaps twenty porters; nevertheless, not only were the principal summits climbed, but a great deal of exploratory work was done in untouched country at the northern end of the range.

Before passing on to our attempt on the peaks, which was the third successful one, it may be well to outline roughly the size and position of Ruwenzori. In the last Ptolemy's guess was not far wrong, for it lies about a half degree north of the equator. The general direction of the range is north and south, and it consists of six snow mountains or groups of peaks separated from each other by lower ridges uncovered by snow. The length of the entire snowy range is about eleven miles;

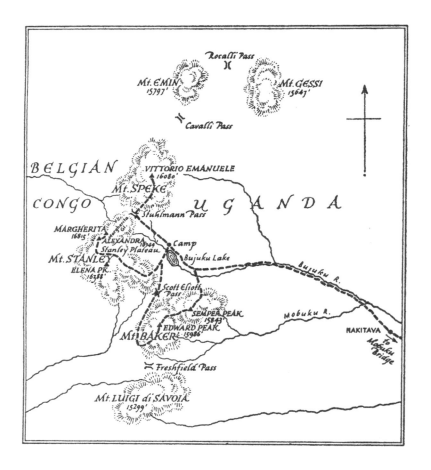

Map 3: Ruwenzori

extending north and south of this are perhaps twenty miles of high but vegetation-covered ridges; and beyond again are the low foothills. At the southern end is Lake Edward, at the northern Lake Albert, and on the western side lies the trough of the western branch of the Great Rift Valley. Flowing through this trough from Lake Edward to Lake Albert is the Semliki River, into which river and its two lakes flows all the drainage from the northern, southern, western, and even eastern slopes of the Ruwenzori massif. Thus the White Nile issuing from Lake Albert is fed almost entirely by the waters from Ruwenzori, while Lake Victoria and the Victoria Nile is altogether a separate and independent system.

Another remarkable fact is that, although the range constitutes the most considerable group of snow mountains in Africa, a group situated in the middle of the continent and running in the direction of the main axis, yet it does not form part of the main watershed. The divide between the Nile and Congo drainage systems lies west of the Semliki River and is the western escarpment of the Great Rift. It is prolonged southwards through the Mfumbiro volcanoes and the west shore of Lake Kivu.

Of the six groups into which the range is divided the greatest is that of Mount Stanley, which includes four peaks over 16,000 feet, amongst them the two highest, Margherita and Alexandra. Mount Speke has two peaks, both over 16,000 feet; Mount Baker comes next with Edward Peak, 15,988 feet, and Semper, 15,843 feet. North of these are the two groups of Mount Emin and Mount Gessi, comprising four peaks of about 15,700 feet, and south is Mount Luigi di Savoia, with three peaks of 15,200 feet. The five passes which separate the six groups are, from north to south, Roccati, Cavalli, Stuhlmann, Scott Elliott, and Freshfield. Disregarding the lesser peaks, whose names have not been mentioned, one sees that the early explorers have not been forgotten in the system of nomenclature adopted. The practice of naming mountains after persons is not easily justified. Even a name like Robinson, in the Lakes, sanctified as it is by use, sounds incongruous amongst such as Scafell, Saddleback, Fairfield, and many more equally beautiful. In extenuation here it may be urged that there are almost certainly no native names for individual peaks, many of which are not visible from the lower slopes where the natives live.

The snows of Ruwenzori: An air photograph

The Italian expedition confirmed the observations of Stuhlmann and Scott Elliott that there was no possibility of a volcanic origin for these mountains, a fact which is the more surprising because around the base of the chain to the south and east are many traces of volcanic activity. Dotted about among the eastern foothills are numerous crater lakes, which form delightful turquoise-coloured gems in a rich green forest setting. Hippos love these secluded little lakes, while the surrounding forest is the home of a wonderful variety of birds and animals—animals both small and great, of which last class the rhinoceros alone is absent. Here, then, are traces of volcanic action, but to the south are volcanoes themselves—the Mfumbiro volcanoes, of which one is still active. Surrounding these are many miles of lava-covered ground with numerous crater lakes. To the north and east of Ruwenzori earth tremors are frequent, and of the few days I have spent at Fort Portal not one has passed without an earth tremor of some kind.

The glaciers of the range are small and are gradually receding. They have no real basins, but resemble icecaps from which depend numerous ice-streams. The most striking feature of the snow regions is the number of the cornices, most of which assume an appearance peculiar to this region. The formation looks very like a section of an ostrich feather fan. None of the glaciers descend lower than 14,000 feet, the snow-line being 700 feet or 800 feet higher. Above 14,000 feet rain generally falls as snow, but does not lie long.

Any traveller familiar with snow mountains is quick to notice two unusual features of Ruwenzori's glacial streams. They are comparatively small and, owing to an absence of the usual detritus, are very clean. Much melting of the glaciers is no doubt prevented by the almost permanent mist which covers the range, but that this does take place in some small degree is easily seen from the slight variation in volume of the streams, whose flow gradually rises as the daily sun exercises what slight power it has in these mist-covered regions, and diminishes again at night. The absence of silt is accounted for by the fact that the glaciers are almost stationary, and so grind no detritus from the rocks beneath them, being, as already noticed, more in the form of ice-caps crowning the summits and high ridges than ice-streams flowing down a valley. In spite of this apparently slight degree of melting, a great volume of water flows from the range to feed the White Nile. The range, by reason of its great extent and height, forms a large condenser upon which the hot, moist air drawn up from the surrounding plains is precipitated as snow, mist, or rain. A multitude of valleys scarring the slopes discharge this water again into neighbouring rivers. Stanley counted sixty-two rivers flowing from the mountains into the Semliki from the southern and western slopes alone.

The upper slopes of Ruwenzori, from 10,000 feet to the snow-line, comprise a world of their own—a weird country of moss, bog, rotting vegetation, and mud, on which flourish grotesque plants that seem to have survived from a past era; the vegetation of some lost world inhabited by dinosauria, pterodactyls, and mammoths. Here are seen gaunt giant groundsel crowned at the top with spiky heads like half-eaten artichokes; tough, leafless shrubs with white everlasting flowers called helichrysum; grey, withered, and misshapen tree heaths, tumescent with swollen growths of moss and lichen oozing moisture; monstrous freaks of nature bred from the union of mist and morass; a slimy barrier serving to enhance and make more desirable the fresh purity of the snows which lie beyond.

Such are the Mountains of the Moon—vying not with the austere splendour and sublimity of the Alps or the Himalaya, but by their position, mystery, traditions, and matchless scenery, ranking, surely, amongst the wonders of the world.

CHAPTER VIII

THE APPROACH TO RUWENZORI

A barren detested vale, you see, it is:
The trees, though summer, yet forlorn and lean,
O'ercome with moss, and baleful mistletoe.

—SHAKESPEARE

WE LEFT TURBO BY CAR on the morning of January 9th and, leaving the squat bulk of Mount Elgon on our right, headed for the high granite obelisk seen in the distance marking the position of Tororo, on the Uganda border. The Uganda roads have a well-deserved reputation, so that we sped rapidly along, dropping gradually until Jinja was reached about tea-time.

Jinja is a little town on the shores of Lake Victoria close to the Ripon Falls, where the Nile issues from the lake to begin its long journey to the sea. The falls were discovered by Speke in 1862, who thus solved the problem of the position of one of the Nile sources. They are only about twenty feet high, but even without the romantic associations of the river it is an impressive sight to see the great volume of water sweeping over the falls to run through a gorge and disappear round a wooded bend a mile lower down. Above the falls are pools and shallows in which crocodiles and hippos laze, while immediately below, the water seems to be alive with big Nile perch, 30 lbs. to 40 lbs. in weight, trying ceaselessly but vainly to jump up the falls.

In addition to its romantic situation, Jinja is celebrated for a nine-hole golf-course lying close to the lake shore, the grass of which is kept short by the hippos which emerge nightly from the lake to graze. There is a local rule about hippo foot-marks, which are treated in the same way as rabbit scrapes at home, where the ball can be lifted without penalty. One of these hippos was such a regular visitor that he was known to the people of Jinja, indeed of Uganda and even further, as Horace. A usual way of entertaining visitors was to drive down to the links in the evening to watch Horace enjoying his supper. There was a story current when we were there that one party, which had dined not wisely but too well, went down with the avowed intention of pulling Horace's tail. One of the 'pot valiant,' boldly leaving the car, advanced towards the hippo, but Horace, also feeling playful, came for the man and chased him back to the car, taking a large piece out of something more than the slack of his breeches *en route*. The party were too happy to notice much amiss until someone discovered the presence of quantities of blood, and, after returning hastily to the town, they spent a long time in persuading a doctor that he was not being made the victim of a drunken leg-pull. The upshot was that the would-be humorist spent a month or so in hospital.

Until 1928 the Uganda Railway, so called, perhaps, because it never entered Uganda, stopped at Kisumu, on the east shore of the lake. Now, the main line enters Uganda to the north, crosses the Nile by a bridge just below the Ripon Falls, and terminates at Kampala, eighty miles away. The bridge also carries a road, but before that was built travellers by road were obliged to cross an arm of the lake by a rather cranky ferry running at very infrequent intervals. Thanks to the bridge, no time had to be wasted by us on the ferry, and we pushed on that evening, reaching Kampala at seven after a run of 250 miles.

We were ready for an early start next day in order to cover the remaining 200 miles to Fort Portal in good time, but we were delayed until seven waiting for a mechanic whom we had agreed to take out to a car stranded seventy-five miles out. It was a case of assisting a damsel in distress, so the delay was suffered gladly by one of us, and by the other without impatience.

At four we reached Fort Portal, where we put up at a small hotel. It is the centre of the Toro district of Uganda, a district more favoured by soil and climate than the rest of the Protectorate. The altitude is about 5000 feet, the rainfall well distributed, and the soil a fertile, volcanic ash. Coffee is the main European crop, but bananas, citrus fruits, maize, wheat, potatoes and other vegetables, all flourish. To live in this garden is pleasant and simple, but to earn money from it is a different matter, for its remoteness is a severe handicap. To export anything involves 200 miles of road haulage and 800 miles of rail before one starts paying for sea carriage, so that only high-priced crops can

Ruwenzori: Seventh lake, Nyamgasani Valley

justify themselves, and coffee, unfortunately, can no longer be put in that category.

Outside the township, on a neighbouring eminence, are the houses which comprise the palace of the King of Toro, or the Kabaka, who rules his country with the assistance of a Prime Minister and a Council of Elders, advised when necessary by the District Commissioner, who lives in Fort Portal. The thatching of the houses of the palace and the neat reed fences surrounding them are evidently the work of real craftsmen.

Fort Portal lies at the northern end of the Ruwenzori range, and only two miles north-west is the brink of the steep escarpment which plunges down 2000 feet to the floor of the Western Rift Valley, through which the Semliki River winds. It is called the Semliki, but it is in reality the head waters of the White Nile. Across the bare, brown, sun-scorched plain at the bottom, broken only by the silver coils of the river, is the steep opposing wall of the Rift, crowned on top with the outer fringes of the Congo forest and forming the Congo-Nile divide, the watershed of Africa.

We spent a busy morning buying blankets, cooking-pots, and cigarettes for the porters, and interviewing the District Commissioner, from whom we got a letter to a native chief, who lived at the entrance to the Mobuku Valley, invoking his aid. Which things done, we drove south for 45 miles, reaching the Mobuku River at midday.

We hoped to find our chief somewhere in the neighbourhood, but the task promised to be difficult, for, to our surprise, the whole of the native population of Uganda seemed to be gathered there. We learnt that a bridge across the Mobuku was being built; an operation that had been in progress for the past two years. Several times it had almost reached completion, only to be washed away by the river coming down in flood. That day H.E. the Governor of Uganda, who was on tour, had come in person to inspect progress; hence the assembled multitude.

Contrary to all expectations, we did find the needle in the haystack of humanity and gave the chief the D.C.'s letter, but that was all, for under the circumstances we could not expect to receive much attention.

We had another stroke of luck when we found amongst the crowd at the bridge a local settler, or, since he was the only one, *the* local settler. He lived a few miles up the Mobuku Valley, and he it was who had been Dr Humphreys's companion in 1926. We were invited to make his house our headquarters and offered every assistance.

The farm was seven miles away, whither we at once proceeded along a very narrow and tortuous farm track. Driving away from the vicinity of the bridge when it was apparently the duty of everyone to be present, we had the guilty feeling of playing truant, while even the car registered a protest by puncturing a tyre. While we were perspiringly jacking it up to effect a change, two very smart and impressively large cars came round a bend, the leading one flying a small Union Jack. By pulling off the road a little they could have squeezed past, but we realised that this was hardly to be expected, so, fearful of delaying the ceremony at the bridge and feeling like the blundering hero of some Bateman drawing—the bluejacket who spat on the quarter-deck—we hastily kicked the jack away to manhandle the car off the road into the bush. It was a good car, but we blushed for its dingy paint and battered wings festooned with kit, and as the gubernatorial procession filed past in slow and shining solemnity it seemed to us that the bush was the only place for it.

Rather shaken by this little incident, we finished changing the wheel, and pushed on, only abandoning the car where the road came to an abrupt end below a steep hill. On top of this hill were some thatched huts belonging to the farm, and, having procured some boys to assist with the baggage, we toiled up to them.

The D.C.'s letter bore fruit. Very early next morning there arrived at the huts a great crowd of volunteers eager to accompany us, indeed, we had difficulty in persuading them that we wanted only a few. After much haranguing on both sides we picked out fourteen of the toughest-looking and finally got away about midday. Thirteen of the men carried 50-lb. loads, while the duty of the other was to go ahead with a panga (a heavy bush knife) to open up the overgrown track.

Some of these natives, Bakonjo, living on the lower slopes of the mountain knew what lay ahead, as they had been up to about 13,000 feet, with previous parties. They were a cheerful, willing lot, as tough as they looked, and well suited to carrying 50-lb. loads over the difficult country we presently reached. They had little equipment and less clothing, and were delighted to receive the blanket and vest issued to

Ruwenzori: First glimpse of the snows from the Mobuku Valley

Ruwenzori: Sunset over the Congo from the Stanley Plateau

them out of the expedition's slender resources. Their most treasured personal possessions, chief of which was a pipe and tobacco, were carried in a little fur pouch slung from the neck. Another very important item of equipment carried by many was a cigar-shaped package of leaves closely wrapped and bound up against the weather. Inside was a sort of moss or lichen, which seemed to have the faculty of smouldering away happily without any air for days on end. When a light was wanted, the package was unwrapped and a few breaths soon blew the smouldering tinder to life.

The day was fine and hot as we marched through banana groves by the river before ascending a steep and narrow spur to a camping-ground called Bihunga. This was a small level spot on top of the spur at an altitude of about 7000 feet.

Here cultivation ceases, and 1000 feet higher thick forest is reached. Before burying ourselves in this, we stopped for a last look at the outside world to see beyond the green foothills a wide, flat expanse of light brown, almost yellow, country, a monotony of colour only relieved by the pale blue of a distant lake. The whole was bounded by the gentle, rounded summits of the Ankole Highlands. The sun still shone, but on entering the forest we were unaware of it, nor were we to see it again for many days. We climbed steeply to a pleasant little forest clearing called Nakitawa, where we camped. It was only one o'clock, but nothing, not even bribes, would induce the porters to go a step further. We realised there were also disadvantages in having men who had been up before, for they knew the time-honoured camping-grounds and used them in an undeviating ritual, at whatever time they were reached.

From this point it was a matter of fighting one's way rather than marching, and every day the work became more severe. The track—or rather the line we followed, for track there was none—plunged headlong into deep valleys, only to climb the opposing slope with uncompromising abruptness. The Mobuku was already behind us, and now we crossed its greater tributary the Bujuku, up the valley of which our route lay.

Overhead, tall trees wrapped about with a tangle of creepers formed a dense canopy which shut out the light; underfoot was a matted carpet of undergrowth—ferns, brambles, fallen bamboos, giant nettles (said to be capable of making even an elephant sit up), and dead trees—over which we sometimes crawled, sometimes crept beneath on all fours, and sometimes had to cut a way through with the panga. The pace was painfully slow, but it was something that the porters could advance at all, balancing their loads on their heads, walking barefoot along the green and slimy trunk of some fallen giant many feet above the ground, or lowering themselves down steep and slippery cliffs of earth; torn by thorns, snatched at and caught by creepers, stung by nettles, plastered with mud, and everlastingly wet.

Through a window in the living green wall of our prison we saw for a brief moment the ice peaks of Stanley and Speke, filling the head of the valley, before they vanished once more in wreathing cloud. From now on 'Ruwenzori weather' prevailed, so that, but for one other occasion, this was the only time the peaks revealed themselves to us between dawn and sunset.

We camped that night under a dripping, overhanging cliff at about 9500 feet at almost the upper limit of the forest zone. As forest it compared ill with the clean, straight-growing cedar and the podocarpus giants of the Mau or the forested slopes of Mount Kenya, for a few indifferent podocarpus were the only trees that looked as if they would make timber. The forest zone is succeeded in turn by a short but dense belt of bamboo, and then, above 10,000 feet, by a forest of tree heaths. This is a thick stand of leafless trees of a uniform height of twenty to thirty feet, made unnatural and grotesque by waving beards of lichen hanging from every branch and twig, and by the tumid mossy growths covering the trunks.

The going, however, was very much better in this forest of tree heath. The gradient was slight, with little to hinder progress except the soft and spongy ground, so that the camping-place of Kigo was reached by midday. We were welcomed by a cold drizzle, which made the porters the more resolute to stop where they were in spite of our protests at the shortness of the march.

Beyond the tree heaths we found an even stranger country, where solid earth disappeared altogether under an overburden of moss or fallen and rotting giant groundsel (senecio). Thick groves of these grow on every hand; they are from twelve to twenty feet high, and thick in proportion, but can easily be pushed over with one hand, so that in the groves themselves there are many more trees lying than standing. So rotten are these fallen trunks that they will not support the weight of a man, with the result that forcing a path through the labyrinth presented by senecio forest, growing as it does out of a morass, is laborious to the point of exhaustion.

By way of variety one can make a less slimy but perhaps more strenuous way through the suggestively named 'helichrysum' bushes; this a pink and white flowered 'everlasting,' growing nearly as high as a man. It is stiff, tough, wiry, trying to both clothes and temper. Its pretty flowers, like coloured paper, which do a little to brighten a drab landscape, make insufficient amends for a harsh, stubborn, unyielding nature. Over all a clammy mist hangs like a pall, and a deep silence broods. Even the innumerable brooks and rivulets are hushed as they flow deep below ground level in a narrow trench of moss—moss that seems to breed wherever the mist touches, on tree, plant, earth, or rock.

Such was the nightmare landscape across which we toiled on our fifth day, and such is the nature of all the high valleys below the snow-line, giving to Ruwenzori a mystery and strange beauty that has not its likeness in any other land. A country that only the language of Lewis Carroll could paint, the natural habitat of Snarks and Jabberwoks and jub-jub birds. A slough, but not a Slough of Despond, for were not the Delectable Mountains at hand?

CHAPTER IX

THE ASCENT OF RUWENZORI

Round its breast the rolling clouds are spread.

—GOLDSMITH

WE CAMPED IN A DAMP but welcome cave at about 13,000 feet, hard by the Bujuku Lake, a mournful, shallow mere which, with its foetid, mud-lined shores, was in harmony with the desolate landscape surrounding it. But from the cave our eyes lingered, not on this, but on the grim precipices across the valley below the snows of Mount Baker, on the serrated ridge of the Scott Elliott Pass, and the peaks and glaciers of Mount Stanley. This, however, was a view which was seldom, if ever, seen in whole except for a minute or so at dawn or dusk, so that we were usually compelled to trust to fleeting glimpses of rock and ice, peak and ridge, seen through the writhing mists, and in imagination link the whole together.

Our first plan had been to carry all our own food and kit to an advance base near the Scott Elliott Pass—a pass lying between Mount Stanley and Mount Baker which we hoped would give us access to both mountains. It was some time before the mist cleared sufficiently for us to identify the pass, and from that distance it looked as though the approach to it might prove too much for our porters. We had already sent eight of these down, retaining six with us in the cave. They were comfortable enough and moderately content, but were so daunted by the appearance of things higher up that it seemed advisable to leave them out of our calculations and shift for ourselves. On account, therefore, of this alteration in our plans the afternoon of our arrival at the cave was a busy one, sorting out food and kit for ourselves for five days, and making it up into two loads of 40 lbs. We intended to establish our camp on the Stanley plateau, from there climb Margherita and Alexandra, move our bivouac nearer to Mount Baker and climb that before returning to the cave to refit. We had yet to discover that as the hare must first be caught, so, on Ruwenzori, the peak must first be found.

We left camp at eight on the morning of the 17th, with two men carrying our loads. Skirting the lake-shore, we climbed through senecios, reached the rocks, and at about 15,000 feet came upon the site of a former bivouac. It was now eleven o'clock, and, as snow was beginning to fall, we sent the men back to the cave, shouldered our 40-lb. packs, and climbed slowly upwards. About one o'clock we reached the foot of the Elena Glacier, and, climbing now on snow at an easy angle, we presently reached the yet flatter slopes of the Stanley Plateau. The weather was thick, so that our sole guides were infrequent glimpses of the rocks of the Elena and Moebin Peaks close on our left. By three o'clock we were completely at a loss as to our whereabouts, so we pitched our little tent in what we imagined was a sheltered spot, and prayed for the mist to lift. At sunset the longed-for clearing came, showing, to our amazement, our camp pitched almost on the divide.

A few hurried steps up a snow-slope, and we were brought to a stand as much by a view which held us spellbound as by the sudden falling away of the ground at our feet. Far to the west and below us, through a rift in the driving clouds, we could see the dark green, almost black, carpet of the Congo Forest, upon whose sombre background was traced a silvery design by the winding Semliki River. To the south showed a lighter patch, where the waters of Lake Edward reflected the last light of day; but in a moment sinking sun and rising mist merged all but the snow at our feet in a once more impenetrable gloom.

Of more practical value to us than this wonderful sight was the exposure for a brief minute of a snow ridge to the north leading up to a peak which we knew must be Alexandra. In spite of the conditions, we had pitched camp in a position well placed for an attempt on this peak, and we turned in with unjustified complacence, for it was more by good luck than good management. It snowed all night and was still snowing at dawn, so that the clearing from which we had hoped to refresh our memories never came. When we started at 7.30 to try to 'hit off' the ridge which we had seen the previous evening, visibility was limited to about ten yards, and, after wandering perplexedly for two hours amongst a maze of crevasses, we returned to camp. Caution was needed, as tracks were obliterated by fresh snow almost as soon as they were made.

The persistent snow soon found the weak spots in our little tent, which was not well adapted either for sheltering two men or for use on snow. Pools of water soon accumulated on the floor, limiting the area at our disposal, an area already made small by an inconvenient centre pole, so that it became increasingly difficult to keep our sleeping-bags dry. In the evening another clearing in the mist caused us to dash out, but we only got as far as the foot of the ridge before gathering darkness compelled us to return.

On the third day it was still misty but the snow had stopped falling. Assisted by our tracks of the previous night, which in places were still visible, we reached the ridge and began climbing. Except for one awkward cornice and the uncertain quality of the snow, the climb was not difficult, the summit (16,749 feet) being reached by midday. There was a patch of rock on top where we found a cairn in which were records left by the Duke of the Abruzzi in 1906 and Dr Humphreys in 1926. We sat there till 2.30 p.m., but caught only passing glimpses of the neighbouring summit of Margherita. Camp was reached at 4 p.m., when a brief clearing enabled us to wring out our sleeping-bags and bale the tent. Our success on Alexandra, combined at sunset with another remarkable view of the Congo and a sight of the Margherita ridge, sent us to bed in a more or less contented frame of mind.

More snow fell in the night, but we turned out at 7.30 a.m. and were rewarded by seeing Margherita clearly for five minutes. By the time we had got under way, the mist had re-gathered, so that in a short time our ideas as to position and direction became as nebulous and woolly as the mist itself. The crevasses seemed more numerous and the mist thicker than on our first attempt, but, after groping about for some hours, we saw looming before us what was undoubtedly a ridge.

At the foot of it was a steep rock buttress, which we managed to turn on the right, traversing back above it to the left. Hopes ran high as we reached the crest of the ridge and began to follow it, but next moment we stood dumbfounded, staring, Crusoe-like, at footprints in the snow. Such was our bewilderment that wild and impossible conjectures of another party on the mountain flashed across our minds before we realised the unflattering truth that these were our

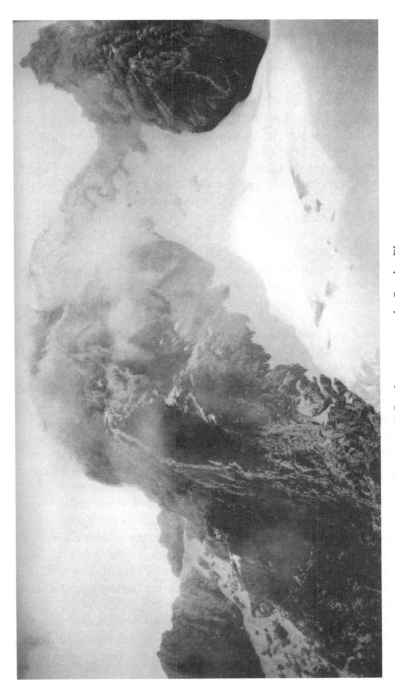

Ruwenzori: On the way up to the Stanley Plateau

tracks of the previous day, and that we were climbing Alexandra for the second time.

We crept back to camp with our tails well down, to pass a rather miserable night, depressed as much by our failure as by the state of the tent, whose contents, including our sleeping-bags, were now sopping wet. Our food was almost finished, but before our forced descent on the morrow we determined to have a final crack at Margherita.

By three in the morning we were so cold in our wet sleeping-bags that we gave up trying to sleep, brewed some tea, and prayed for dawn. Camp was struck, the sodden loads packed, and at six we moved off down the glacier, dumping the loads near the foot of the Stanley Plateau. Then, in a last desperate resolve to find the Margherita ridge, we turned north again. The usual mist prevailed, while the width and frequency of unbridged crevasses made vain any attempt at following a compass course, which in any case could only have been an approximation.

These repeated changes of direction enforced on us by the crevasses tried our tempers severely; every change gave rise to heated argument, during which each of us would fall to drawing little maps in the snow with ice-axes to illustrate our respective theories.

Once more a rock buttress loomed up. It was viewed with suspicion and tackled without enthusiasm, while every moment we expected to come once again upon our old tracks. In this we were delighted to be disappointed, and at eleven o'clock we reached the summit of an undoubted peak, but which we could not tell. It was snow-covered, so there could be no records to find; all to be done was to wait for the mist to clear. This we did, sitting in a hollow scraped in the snow.

The climb had been an interesting one but not difficult. The ridge and the summit were draped with cornices of a strangely beautiful feathery appearance. Very little melting appears to take place at these heights, so it is possible that this formation is due to wind rather than rapid alterations in temperature. On the other hand, the presence of numbers of large ice stalactites under the cornices suggests a considerable range of temperature.

Unless another night without food was to be spent on the glacier, our departure had to be timed for 3 p.m. A searching wind began to lessen our interest as to what peak we were on, threatening to drive us off its summit with our knowledge unsatisfied. Time after time the swirling mists seemed to be thinning. Repeatedly we would take off our snow-glasses in the hope of finding a tangible clue in the sea of fog, only to be baulked by fresh clouds rolling up from some apparently inexhaustible supply. Repeatedly we were disappointed, but at last a clearing came. It lasted hardly a minute, but it was long enough for us to see and recognise the familiar summit of Alexandra, and to realise from its relative position that we must be on Margherita (16,815 feet).

It was sheer luck to have hit off the ridge on such a day, so that we were almost jubilant as we started down. Helped by our outgoing tracks, we reached our rucksacks at 4.30 p.m., and, stopping only to swallow a mouthful of raw pemmican, we hit out for the cave. In spite of mist and gathering gloom we found the route, quitted the snow for the rocks, slid and slithered down moss-grown slabs, and soon were fighting our way through the senecios above the lake. Burdened as we were with water-logged packs and exhausted by our previous efforts, our condition was such that our progress was governed more by the impulse of gravity than by our legs. So with one mind we steered straight for the mud of the lake-shore, knowing that it would be soft, but doubting whether a quicksand itself could be worse than the senecio toils in which we were struggling.

It was not a quicksand, but a very fair imitation, and, withal, very evil-smelling; 'Here, therefore, they wallowed for a time, being very grievously bedaubed with dirt; and Christian, because of the burden that was on his back, began to sink into the mire.' Frying-pan and fire, devil and deep sea, Scylla and Charybdis, all seemed weak comparisons for the horns of our dilemma. Finally we took once more to the senecio forest—perhaps because it did not smell—and by nightfall reached the cave and the welcome warmth of a roaring fire.

Although, on the march, no words could be bad enough for the senecio, or giant groundsel, in camp we sang a different tune. To all appearances it looks as likely to burn as cabbage-stalk, but, dead or alive, wet or dry, it burns almost as well as birchwood. Without it life in the high valleys of Ruwenzori, where the sun is hardly ever seen and where to move a yard from camp is to be soaked, would be almost unbearable; at any rate to natives, to whom sitting over a fire, or even in the smoke of a fire, is meat and drink.

Ruwenzori: The summit of Alexandra

After devoting a day to food and rest, and the drying of clothes and sleeping-bags, we set out for Mount Speke in thick weather on January 23rd. As it lies to the north of the Bujuku Lake, our line of march lay up the valley towards the Stuhlmann Pass at its head. In an attempt to cut short the struggle with vegetation and morass we tried to break out of the valley by climbing the cliffs of its eastern flank, but we were repulsed by the moss-covered slabs. After several great strips of moss had peeled away, almost taking us with them, we continued up the valley, at last reaching the snow above the pass. We roped up, more from ingrained orthodoxy than necessity, and climbed an easy snow slope to Vittorio Emmanuele (16,080 feet), gaining its summit at half past ten. From this vantage-point, almost the centre of the range, we should have seen, but for the mist, most of the snow peaks and their glaciers. For three hours we sat there waiting patiently for a clearing. At half past one the mist did lift a little, giving us a glimpse of a summit along the ridge to the north, which appeared to be higher than ours. Whether it was so or not, it gave us an excuse for getting warm, so we raced off along the ridge, climbed three small intervening hillocks, and reached the top of the fourth unnamed peak. Dr Humphreys was of the opinion that this summit was higher than Vittorio, which is officially the highest, an opinion with which we were inclined to agree. The point is only of academic interest, however, for not one of the four is worthy of the name of 'peak.'

We started back at half past two in a curious mixture of thunder and snow, reaching camp in two hours. We tried more short cuts on the way, and at least had the melancholy satisfaction of proving once again that if mossy slabs are not ideal for ascents, they are excellent for descents, if effortless speed is the main consideration.

Our six porters, who were in a fair way to becoming troglodytes, began to hope that the madness which had driven us to these inhospitable wastes had now spent itself, and that with a return to sanity there would be a return to a warmer climate. Whether man could be eternally happy in the heaven, paradise, or nirvana offered by the several religions has always seemed to me doubtful (for, after all, bliss is only appreciated after spells of misery), and here were these natives, enjoying what I imagine to be a native's idea of heaven, with nothing to do but eat, drink, sleep, and draw their pay, and yet counting the days until they could return to work, women, and taxation. Since the only obligation they were under was to remain passive, and desertion would involve being active, it was not difficult to persuade them to wait a little longer, as we were able to assure them that one more day would suffice to exorcise the devil which possessed us.

That day, January 24th, we proposed to devote to the climbing of Mount Baker direct from our base camp—a much more formidable task than the climbing of Speke although it was the lower of the two, being only 15,986 feet. Our original plan had been to attempt it by the ridge, leading up from the Scott Elliott Pass, but the shattered, ice-glazed rocks of that ridge presented a very forbidding appearance. The alternative was to climb it by the north face from a point in the Bujuku Valley lower than our camp site. We started very early to see what we could do.

'Reculer pour mieux sauter' may sometimes be sound strategically, but it calls for high morale in those called upon to practise it, and there is no more trying a way of starting an ascent than by a descent. Our route began with a descent of the valley for a good half-mile. It was not as though we could just run down. On the contrary, every foot of it had to be fought for in the depressing knowledge that every foot so gained was a foot lost on the mountain, so that it was with mingled feelings of relief and dismay that we at last found ourselves at the foot of the lower cliffs of Baker, which bound the south side of the valley, faced by a climb of what was now more than 3000 feet. The lower part of the cliffs were, of course, sheathed in moss, a fact which, after our experiences of yesterday, caused us to approach them with misgiving and climb them with caution, the more so because we knew it was seldom possible to safeguard the party with a rope belay. As we slowly gained height, the moss gave place to less treacherous but more difficult ice-glazed rock, while the mist clinging to the face made it impossible for us to choose the best line of ascent. Just below the crest of the east ridge of Baker the rocks steepened. Several attempts were made before we finally overcame these, and, after four hours of continuous climbing, hoisted ourselves on to the snow-covered ridge.

Turning westwards, we followed the ridge at an easy angle over three lesser summits, reaching Semper Peak (15,843 feet) at about one o'clock. Here we found a cairn containing the records of the

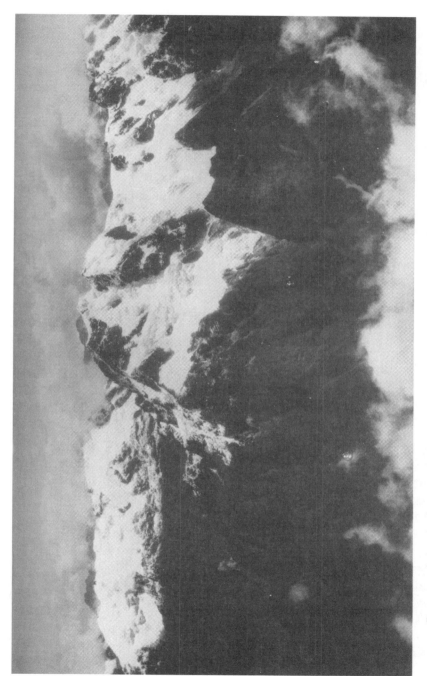

Ruwenzori: An air photograph showing Mount Stanley in foreground, and Mount Baker, in the distance

all-too-thorough Italian party, but we derived some satisfaction from having made a new route. To the south, a quarter of a mile away, was the top, Edward Peak (15,986 feet), and almost as we reached it we enjoyed the novel and pleasing experience of the mists melting away in the middle of the day. Looking across to the Stanley Plateau, where we had played at Blind Man's Buff for four days with Alexandra and Margherita, we found it difficult to imagine that anyone could have had any trouble in finding them. The whole scene stood revealed, and took on a fresh aspect in this almost unnatural sunlight. As dawn dispels the weird shapes and half-seen horrors of the night, so the Mobuku Valley became a smooth and smiling pleasance; the vile tangle of its spongy floor became a firm green lawn, the dark and desolate waters of the mere sparkled gaily, the slimy mud of its shores looked like hard yellow sand. The snow peaks themselves took on a milder aspect, and with the clouds filling and blotting out the lower valleys, which might have destroyed the illusion by their emptiness, we might have been amongst one of the homely lesser ranges of the Alps, instead of the mysterious Mountains of the Moon.

Encouraged by this fair scene, and momentarily forgetful, perhaps, of what the smiling faces of the valleys concealed, we planned an ambitious return journey by a complete traverse of Mount Baker, with a descent towards the Freshfield col which divides Mount Baker from Luigi di Savoia, the southernmost peak. From the col we would drop down into the unnamed valley between Mount Baker and Mount Stanley, on the south side of the Scott Elliott Pass, returning to the Bujuku Valley and our camp over this last-named pass. It meant a long day, and was rather a shot in the dark, but it took us into fresh country, and, in spite of the prudent adage, we preferred the unknown to the known evils of the mossy slabs up which we had come.

After half an hour's rest on the summit we began the descent of the south ridge towards Freshfield col at about two o'clock. Realising too well that every step south was taking us further from home and lengthening our forthcoming struggle in the valley, we decided to cut matters short by descending from the ridge into the valley before reaching the col. The steeper snow below the ridge lay insecurely on top of ice and needed care, but we were soon off the glacier, encountering the less obvious but greater perils of steep rock covered with a type of moss new to our experience, which was almost imperceptible. The rock itself looked bare, and seemed reasonably trustworthy, until a sudden skid provoked closer inspection and revealed the presence of the new enemy.

The slope which fell away at our feet was steep and convex, so that we could not see what lay between us and the valley floor. In the nature of things some sort of steep wall was to be expected near the bottom, and so it was found. It was so steep that but for the assistance of the hated helichrysum which grew out of it we could never have tackled it, and must have returned to the ridge to descend by the much longer way of the Freshfield col. The helichrysum grew in profusion on the face of the cliff, clinging there with all the toughness and tenacity that we knew so well and had so often cursed—a toughness we now had occasion to bless. It was at once an enemy and friend; one moment we were reviling it as heartily as ever for holding us back, and the next giving thanks as we used it for a 'Thank-God-handhold' in the descent of some steep rock wall. But for its aid many such places would have defeated us, while the only toll it exacted was for me the loss of a wrist-watch and for S. a sprained shoulder.

Once we were down on the valley floor there began what we had expected and feared—a long fight against giant groundsel, helichrysum, chaotic boulders, and the approach of night. The valley was closely shut in between the high containing walls of the lower cliffs of Mount Baker and Mount Stanley. Debris falling from the slopes of these mountains filled the valley, and in one place had dammed it to form two lifeless tarns which deepened the melancholy aspect of this grim defile.

Approaching the foot of the Scott Elliott Pass, the impeding vegetation gave way to scree, but we had to summon all our flagging energies in an effort to reach the col quickly, to see something of our way down the other side before darkness descended and left us benighted. We pressed on, and, as we topped the ridge, there was just light enough to see the Bujuku Lake below, and at our feet a narrow gully which seemed to offer a practicable route.

Hurrying down this as fast as safety permitted, we joined battle once more with senecio forest and helichrysum, in which I suffered the additional loss of my camera and the irreplaceable exposed film which it contained. We reached the lake-shore in a darkness which, though 'hellish,' did not 'smell of cheese,' like the cupboard which the half-drunk James Pigg thrust his head into in mistake for the window. I smelt instead like a sewer as we began floundering along the margin of the lake, sinking to our knees in the noisome mud at every step. On this occasion we preferred it to the senecio, and resigned ourselves, more or less happily, to long wallowing in the slough, because with the water to guide us we were sure of our direction. Presently a boy who had heard our shouts met us with a lamp, and in a short time we were sitting by the fire discussing food and the day's adventures.

In the morning we packed up and bade farewell to the friendly cave which we had come to look upon as home, so warm was its welcome on our belated returns from long, wet days. By promising the porters extra baksheesh we persuaded them to double march all the way, for our road lay downhill and the trail was already broken. They were eager to get back certainly, but it needed a pretty strong incentive to goad them into this fierce activity.

Their labours finished, these six worthies received, besides the blankets and clothes, eleven shillings each, with which they were well pleased. A full month's work on farm or road would not have brought them in as much as this, the fruits of only sixteen days' absence. Now they could return in affluence to their villages, willing and able to astonish the stay-at-homes with tales of hardship and peril amidst the mysterious snows.

The boy we had deputed to keep an eye on the car, left by the road-side, met us with the news that all was well. This was a great relief, because it was quite on the cards that some elephant had stepped on it or that it had been destroyed by a bush fire. Not only was all well with it, but, according to the boy, rather better than well, because a swarm of bees had settled in the box-body. He was surprised when we told him that we did not want them, that we did not even want the car so long as the bees were in possession, but that we would come along again as soon as the present tenants had left. I had experienced swarms of bees in cars before, and I have yet to own a car that will go fast enough in these circumstances.

We were not there to see what wiles he employed to eject them, but when we got down later the swarm had gone but for a few bewildered stragglers. Most natives, if not exactly bee-keepers, encourage bees by hanging up hives made from hollowed logs in trees near their huts; while in the forest, they have an extraordinary keen nose for the honey which is often found in hollow trees and crannies in the rocks. Naked as they are, their boldness and indifference to stings when dealing with the rightful owners would startle the gloved and netted apiarist. Before loading up we held a snake inspection, for it has already been recorded how on another occasion a puff adder, one of the deadliest snakes, was found dozing peacefully on the cylinder head.

In spite of the long exposure to sun, rain, and curious natives, the car consented to start, and we bowled along cheerfully to Kampala and home, giving thanks for the twin blessings of snow mountains on the equator and the means of getting to them. It is interesting to recall that the Abruzzi expedition, as recently as 1906, spent more time in getting from Kampala to the foot than we did on the mountains—thanks to a road and a car. Even to such light-hearted coffee-planters as ourselves, the time involved without such transport could not have been spent away from the farm without some twinges of conscience, to say nothing of the extra cost a caravan of porters would have entailed. Delightful though the slow-moving porter safari may be, giving opportunities of seeing the country, the natives, and the game which no traveller by car ever has, it is but a means to an end, and the loss of these things is compensated for by the more memorable days spent in high places, among the solitudes of ice and snow.

CHAPTER X

THE GOLD RUSH

The narrowing lust of gold.

—TENNYSON

U NTIL 1931 THE SEARCH for precious metals in Kenya had attracted little general interest. The accepted theory seemed to be that, in the Highlands at any rate, any valuable minerals that might exist were buried deep beneath great deposits of volcanic soil, so that to look for them was a waste of time. No doubt a few enthusiasts were not so easily put off, but generally more attention was paid to the neighbouring territory of Tanganyika, which was comparatively rich in minerals, and where promising alluvial diggings were already being exploited. In Kenya in 1923 gold was found in the Lolgorien area south of the Sotik, and a mild 'rush' took place to peg claims. In view of the later history of this particular area, it is difficult to understand why this interest so soon evaporated; the majority who went down there returned disgusted, and in only two places was serious development work undertaken. Ten years later it was becoming apparent that those who took part in that rush were as blind as they were easily discouraged.

Early in 1931 reports of rich finds in the Kakamega district, near the north-east corner of Lake Victoria, began to circulate. At first the stories met with the usual scepticism, in spite of the fact that the Colony was then sinking fast into the trough of the depression when people were more inclined to snatch at straws, most of them being in a fair way to financial drowning. The stories continued, losing nothing in the telling, and interest spread so rapidly that in a year or even less there were few people in the Colony who had not either been to Kakamega or joined some syndicate which was prospecting there.

Napoleon has been fathered with a great many trite aphorisms, so no harm will be done in attributing to him another—'Fortune is a fickle jade, so when she knocks at the door be quick to open'—a saying which

S. and I sometimes think we neglected to our cost. A friend whose farm was not far from S.'s was one of the syndicate which made the original discovery at Kakamega, so that during my periodic visits to S. we used to hear a good deal of what was being found there, and still more of what might be found. In our foolishness, or possibly wisdom (for every seeker was not a finder), we accepted these tales with some reserve, chaffing the enthusiastic teller about holes in the ground and the futility of throwing money down them. It was right and proper enough to desert our respective farms for several weeks of mountaineering, but we simply could not afford to waste a week playing at prospecting around Kakamega.

So in a superior way we remained unmoved, even pitying the poor boobs who left their farms to try their luck. In 1932 the excitement became intense, the 'strike' seemed to be extending, and the rush was no longer confined to settlers of Kenya, as people from South Africa, the Rhodesias, and even America had begun to take a hand. Towards the end of that year the population of the 'field' was over a thousand whites—more than the number of farmers in the whole of Kenya—money was flowing into the country, and many companies were being formed. The Government had employed an eminent geologist* to report on the possibilities, and it was the publication of his report in 1932, which recommended, *inter alia*, the opening of other and wider areas to prospectors, that did much to bring this about.

Gold fever is a very infectious complaint, particularly so when the source of infection is comparatively close and easily accessible; here was no ocean to cross, no snow passes, no thirsty desert to overcome, only the trouble of a day's ride in a car. That I was not infected the first year seems to argue the tranquil mind of the philosopher or the apathetic insensibility of a blockhead. For most of the following year I was out of the country, but when I returned towards the end of it to find the Kakamega gold-field now, more than ever, the all-absorbing topic, I was prepared to listen to the voice of the charmer. This more receptive frame of mind was due to no sudden access of wisdom (or foolishness), but because I had given up coffee-planting and was for the moment at a loose end.

---

*   The late Sir Albert Kitson.

I soon learnt that, of the friends and acquaintances I had, sane or less sane, the few who were not already on the spot were financially interested. As related to me casually, I was, at first, rather impressed by the mysterious and important nature of these interests, since in my ignorance I invested the holders of them with the glamour and power commonly associated with the mining magnates of the Rand. Closer enquiry, however, revealed that the majority of holdings consisted of a fractional share in some syndicate whose modest capital of £100 (nominal) was mostly represented by 'call money' which might or, more likely, might not be forthcoming on demand. In all cases, poverty of capital was offset by richness of title, and he would be a cold, calculating, mean-spirited man who questioned the stability or doubted the future prosperity of the 'Find Gold Syndicate,' 'Amalgamated Black Cats,' 'Blue Reefs Consolidated,' and a hundred others similarly named.

Half a dozen friends or a group of neighbouring farms would combine to float one of these, sending the man who had last seen a golden sovereign or knew quartz from coal to the field to commence operations. For the rest, it was very like backing horses; the stakes were not too big, there were a number of attractively named runners from which to choose, and, though the financial results were usually the same, at least one had a longer run for one's money. When the means of the backers were considered (for by now the resources of most people in Kenya were at a very low ebb), it was surprising how long some of these runs did last; but the sanguine hopes of the majority had first to be completely quenched before a halt was called, while the more prudent or less confident had either to meet the calls for more money or make up their minds to cut their losses.

Since I was now drifting without moorings, it was not long before I was drawn into the current which was setting stronger than ever in the direction of the gold-field. I started up-country, flattering myself that I was going into it with my eyes open, and that if it came to throwing money away I was no mean performer and could manage to dispose of my few assets unaided by any fancy-named syndicate.

For those whose notions of a gold rush have been coloured by the Trail of '98, it will be disappointing to hear that in these degenerate days the gold-field was reached either in the speedy and unromantic comfort of a car, or, in those cases where gold-fever temperature had risen to dangerous heights, by the yet swifter aeroplane. If the road was dry it could be reached in a long day's run from Nairobi, but when I, at last, set out to try my luck, rain compelled me to stop a night at Kisumu, on the shore of Lake Victoria. This was formerly a place of some importance, being the terminus of the Uganda Railway and the port for Uganda, to and from which passengers and produce were brought by steamer across the lake. With the extension of the railway to Uganda in 1928, Kisumu lost its importance and retained only its heat, mosquitoes and ramshackle appearance. Now, however, this town, moribund a year ago, had entered upon a new lease of life owing to the fact that it was the nearest station on the railway for the gold-field, which was only forty miles away. Many of the inhabitants of Kisumu had not even to leave home, for the lucky owner of shop or hotel had his gold-mine under his hand. They were reaping a rich harvest from this new field of activity, a harvest well earned by any who had had the hardihood to remain.

The scene at the hotel was animated. Outside stood a row of cars, most of them ready for the knacker's yard, their box-bodies crammed with camp-kit, picks, shovels, and prospecting tools, with a further miscellany slung on running-boards and wings; while inside the bar their owners forgathered to swap the latest rumours and lies from the field. A new gold-field, like a war, breeds rumour 'painted full of tongues,' where facts become lost in a sea of conjecture or impenetrably disguised by distortion and exaggeration. It is commonly said that 'there are three kinds of liars—liars, damned liars, and mining engineers'; for the last 'prospector' might well be substituted, as nowadays the mining engineer's talents in this direction are limited, or have only a negative quality, owing to the conditions under which he works—all companies enjoining upon their employees the silence of a clam.

Among the motley crowd of enthusiasts, amateur and professional, there were the usual accompanying tipsters whose advice was not entirely disinterested. I had not been there five minutes before being buttonholed by a man who was anxious to do me a good turn by selling me some alluvial claims for £500. He was not at liberty to disclose either the names of his partners or the whereabouts of the claims without some tangible proof (£50) of my *bona fides*, but those were details of little moment in view of the wealth of picturesque information placed at my disposal concerning the past earnings of the claims and their potential yield in the future. The hard-bitten air which on entering Kisumu I had tried to assume had evidently not carried conviction—I must have appeared both opulent and innocent.

Next morning I drove out to the field and began a search for the 'Lucky Strike Syndicate,' one of the 'favourites.' I was not thinking of backing it, but I had an introduction to the manager and hoped to acquire some practical knowledge of the ways of the treasure-hunters. The area open to prospecting began about twenty miles out of Kisumu, and one at once began to see on either side of the road numerous 'pegs' (posts carrying galvanised plates on which were painted the details of the claim), and many direction-boards pointing the way to such promising places as the 'Moonshine Reef' or 'De Profundis,' so that the passing mining magnate on the look-out for valuable properties would have no excuse for missing them. Unluckily, the object of my search was more retiring, and many were the potential El Dorados I visited before running it to earth.

I spent three valuable days here obtaining elementary notions of the art of washing a pan of 'dirt,' the first essential for a prospector, and a general insight into conditions on the field.

To late-comers like myself the difficulties in the way of acquiring claims by pegging seemed to be considerable. Almost every available bit of land was taken up, or, if vacant, so hemmed in by claims as to be useless. There was no map to be had showing existing claims, because the officials in charge of survey and registration could not possibly keep pace with the rate at which pegging was being done. According to the mining laws governing 'reef claims,' no pegging could be done unless a 'discovery of gold reef in place' had been made, which meant that before pegging a claim some reef, vein, or 'leader' actually carrying gold had to be found. The ignorant novice, finding almost every square yard pegged, immediately fell to kicking himself for arriving too late on what was seemingly a 'Tom Tiddler's ground.' If traces of gold had been found on every claim pegged, he argued, then the country must be simply oozing gold. But such impressions were deceptive, because this salutary rule had gone by the board, and most of the pegging now in progress was what is termed 'blind'—that is, without the making of any real 'discovery' but in the hopes of making one. The motive behind this was, of course, to gain time, and to prevent anyone else having a look, and was a practice to which there was no effective check.

In the matter of 'alluvial claims,' where the gold is won from the beds of rivers and streams, the rules are different, for a likely strip of river-bank could be claimed and pegged before any work was done on it. All the earlier discoveries had been of alluvial gold, and it was this type of mining that in the first year or two yielded for some lucky people extraordinarily good returns. As by now practically every foot of stream or river was either in process of being worked or had been worked out and abandoned, attention was concentrated on prospecting for reefs—the reefs from which, in theory, all the alluvial gold had come.

The result of this demand for what was no longer to be had put a value on claims *qua* claims, regardless of whether anything had been found on them or not, with the result that the enterprising early birds were reaping their proverbial, if unjust, reward. It was eighteen months now since gold had first been found here, nor had there been any new or startling discoveries to account for the present 'rush'; but it was just before Christmas, and the middle of the dry season, circumstances combining to swell the normal influx with a crowd of curious sightseers who came to scoff and stayed on to dig. Outsiders of all nationalities were there, but the bulk of the prospectors and miners were the farmers, settlers, clerks, and shopkeepers of Kenya, who were the less reluctant to leave their jobs because, in the depressed conditions then prevailing, they had nothing to gain by sticking to farm, shop, or office.

For my own part, staking a claim was less important than finding a place where I could make a home and find occupation for the next few months. It did not take many days of prowling round to convince me that the cheapest way of supplying this modest need of a desirable residence on top of a profitable goldmine was to find some claim-owning friend with whom I could join forces. Since pretty well the whole population were up there, I was pretty sure of finding someone suitable, and after a week my search came to an end.

It was late one evening when I finally tracked down the man I was looking for. To reach his camp I had to abandon the car and ford the

wide Yala River. D. was a man whose sanguine spirit was not easily sub-
dued, a fact which I already knew, so that when I found him stretched
out on his camp-bed I was not surprised to find that his attitude did
not betoken despair but merely that he was feeling the effects of a late
night at whisky poker. This sounded promising, quite in keeping with
the character of the gold-digger which D. could already claim to be. It
would be pleasant to add that D. had settled his gambling debts with
gold-dust and nuggets, but a regard for truth constrains me to admit
that the stakes were the unromantic shillings and cents. My arrival
roused D. from his lethargy, and, hearing what I wanted, he at once
dragged me off to have a look at his claims, although by that time the
sun was almost down.

D. (even he of the elephants), who was a late aspirant for fortune
like myself, had only been there a month. This surprised me, as he was
the type that would be first in the field on a thing like this, and the
last to leave. Moreover, he had previously been part owner of a gold-
mine in Tanganyika, but perhaps that was an experience bitter enough
to enable him to withstand the renewed temptation for so long. Be
that as it may, he had now made up for lost time and had already
pegged a block of ten claims round a 'discovery' which really did show
some 'colour.' What was more, the country for a mile round was still
unpegged, a fact which might have aroused suspicion, but which, in
our ignorance, seemed to be a special dispensation of Providence in
our favour—one of those rare instances when the race was not to the
swift. In addition to these favourable circumstances, he was in the act
of grabbing twenty alluvial claims on the Yala River, which, if size was
any criterion, could easily hold the wealth of the Indies.

We knew each other well, so there was no difficulty in coming to
terms, with the result that before we got back to the tent I was half-
owner of one promising mine, of any others we might take the trouble
to discover, and a collection of picks, shovels, 'pans,' 'dollies,' earth-
augers, and other tools, which the cynic might think were the most
valuable part of our property.

CHAPTER XI

AMATEUR PROSPECTORS

A thirst for gold,
The beggars vice which can but overwhelm
The meanest hearts

—BYRON

THE FORMATION OF THIS NEW and powerful combine, which for the moment we forbore naming, was honoured that night in the usual fashion, and no time was wasted in getting to work. Next morning at dawn the partners went down to the Yala to measure and peg out their alluvial claims. A layer of gravel and sand under both banks was known to be gold-bearing, so presumably the same held good for the gravel under the present river-bed. It was, therefore, only a matter of selecting from the few promising places still unclaimed. Difficulties enough would come later with the working, for the 'pay-dirt' was eight feet below the surface of the banks, while the river itself was a good hundred feet wide and six feet deep. For the present we ignored this, trusting that later someone with sufficient capital would come along to work our claims on a percentage basis, or even buy them outright.

These hopes were never realised. Our claims were examined, but the test bore-holes showed that they were not rich enough to warrant the heavy expenditure necessary to win the gold. On the banks eight feet of overburden had to be removed to reach the underlying gravel, while to reach that in the river-bed itself the river would have had to be diverted. Alterations of the landscape on this scale were not to be undertaken lightly, for, although the man of money might, and in some cases did, say, like another Hotspur proposing to turn the Trent, 'I'll have it so, a little charge will do it,' there was a Glendower in the shape of the Government which, though it did not actually forbid, insisted on the river being restored eventually to its original course and all the excavations filled in when the gold had been won. A hard condition this, unpalatable, and unprofitable to mining Hotspurs, and one which saved more parts of the river than ours from violent hands.

My recollections of that first day are of the junior partner swimming about in the river at one end of one hundred and twenty feet of chain, played by the senior partner, like a tired tunny-fish, of washing pans of 'pay gravel' brought up by the auger from under eight feet of foul-smelling overburden, and finally of returning late to camp through a deluge of rain. It was a hard day but an interesting one, for the kick we got out of watching the specks of gold trailing after the black sand as we 'panned' the gravel more than repaid us for our toil.

After another day or so of this promiscuous bathing and mud-larking, when a thousand feet of both river-banks had been pegged we turned our attention more than willingly to the reef claims—there one could at least keep dry.

These were the claims under which we hoped to expose, by deep trenching or shaft sinking, a body of goldbearing rock. The rock is usually, not necessarily, quartz—that which Spaniards call *madre de oro*, or 'mother of gold'—and the reef may outcrop at the surface or be buried at a depth of hundreds or even thousands of feet. (On the Rand, in the Village Deep Mine, gold is being mined at 7600 feet below ground level.) Near the surface the ore body may be only a few inches thick— what is termed a 'leader' or 'stringer'—but if this is found to be carrying gold it is always worth while following, as it may lead to the mother lode, of which it is an offshoot. If the reef outcrops, well and good, but more usually the only indications to guide one in the search for the reef are bits of quartz lying about on the surface—'floats,' which have to be traced if possible to their sources. Sometimes there are not even any 'floats' to be found, and then samples of the subsoil have to be taken at close intervals to be washed for traces of gold. As the traces in the sample increase or diminish, so the prospector knows whether he is getting 'colder' or 'warmer' in the game of hunting the elusive reef.

D.'s original discovery was an outcrop of rock in which there were thin veins of quartz. Having crushed the rock in a 'dolly' (an iron pestle and mortar) and having washed the fine sand so obtained in a prospector's pan, one got a fair-sized 'tail' of gold; that is to say, a fine streak of the yellow metal tailing behind the residual sand owing to its greater weight, and showing up unmistakably against the black bottom of the pan. Perhaps not 'unmistakably,' as I remember one sample of quartz which showed tremendous 'tails' of some heavy yellow stuff—a find which made us almost sleepless with excitement until an assay showed it to be, not gold, but some metal of no value.

However, there was no deception about this first discovery, from the quartz veins of which gold was found in every sample, with 'tails' of sufficient size to fill us with the wildest hopes. Unfortunately, the quartz veins, which were few and small, petered out very quickly; nor did we ever succeed in finding the reef from which they must have come.

This early and very partial success went to our inexperienced heads. We did not realise its unsubstantial nature, and so left a more thorough investigation to the future, while we embarked upon a policy of 'pegging' as much of the surrounding unclaimed country as we could, with the object of having something worth while to offer the company which, we confidently expected, would sooner or later come along. This area was all part of a vast tract pegged by a man who later found that he had swallowed more than he could digest, and who for some reason, probably financial, had failed to register the claims. This meant that he had no rights over them, with the result that several people, including D., had taken advantage of his faulty title.

We were so confident of the latent possibilities that we regarded every chance white man who showed himself in the neighbourhood as a dangerous rival—an object of suspicion and hatred. Our days were laborious, our nights uneasy. Christmas Day itself brought to us neither peace nor goodwill, for on the previous evening we had happened upon the 'discovery peg' of some wandering Dutchman, which so wrought upon us that we proclaimed our 'goodwill toward men' by searching feverishly for something to justify the placing of a 'discovery peg' close to his, so as to prevent his encroaching any further on what we regarded as our preserves. Thus did the gold bug arouse the envy, hatred, and malice of two mild, kindly disposed coffee-planters, for I think we were quite prepared to jump his claim, shoot him, and bury him in his own trench had we not already sampled his 'discovery' and found it barren.

Our daily routine was to leave camp at daybreak armed with an entrenching-tool, a geologist's hammer, a magnifying-glass, and a pan, and accompanied by two boys carrying pick, shovel, earth-auger, and food. An eye-witness might well have mistaken us for a party of gravediggers attending the funeral of one of their fellows. We proceeded with bowed head and measured step, our eyes glued to the ground searching for likely looking stones. Quite literally, no stone was left unturned. Any arousing interest were broken, to be examined with the magnifying-glass for traces of free gold. The promising bits of quartz were put in separate bags, with notes as to where they had been found, before being taken home for crushing and testing. The note specifying the place of origin was important, because more experienced prospectors than ourselves had been known to carry home a load of samples, prove one to be carrying gold, and then find themselves unable to remember its place of origin. The methodical examination of every piece of quartz with the pocket lens for visible gold was a rite seldom omitted, and, although none was ever seen, the search never lost its interest or excitement. But the most exciting part of the day came when, back in camp, all the samples were crushed and panned. This was the decisive test, for quartz may be rich in gold and yet show no trace of it even under a magnifying-glass. We worked sitting on boxes outside the tent, one of us pounding away at the quartz in the iron 'dolly,' the other carefully washing the fine dust in the pan. Usually, of course, silence or a groan of despair showed the result to be negative, but occasionally a triumphant yell announced the presence of a 'speck' or, rarely enough, a palpable 'tail' amongst the fine black sand in the pan.

This washing and crushing had to be done with scrupulous care. It was easy to overlook specks, but easier still to see some that were not there. Neglect to clean very thoroughly after each trial the dolly, pestle, sieve, and pan was a fruitful source of trouble. Specks of gold from one successful sample might be left over and turn up again in the next, which, though in reality completely barren, was now made to appear gold-bearing. Much extra work and eventual disappointment were the result, because at least ten more negative tests were necessary before the culprit was compelled to admit that he was the victim of his own carelessness, and that the successful pan had been unwittingly 'salted' by himself.

If a sample giving a 'colour' was found, the procedure was to return to the place next day to try to discover from where the bits of surface quartz or 'floats' had come. If they appeared to lie more plentifully in one particular spot than another, a long narrow trench running at right angle to the general 'strike' of the field would be sunk, in the hope of cutting the reef itself or being directed to it by the finding of some 'leader' or 'stringer.' As previously explained, these are the narrow veins of quartz an inch to eighteen inches thick which at some geologically distant period welled up to the surface from the molten reef below.

It is a fascinating game—so fascinating that even after months and years of continual disappointment a trivial find will fire the prospector afresh with all his old enthusiasm. It is a game which is often played out under conditions of extreme heat, cold, and discomfort. Not that we had much to complain about on that score, for, although we were on the equator, we were 5000 feet above sea level, and the heat was by no means unbearable.

The country in which we thus 'fossicked' about was thickly populated and well cultivated—two factors which made prospecting easier in some respects. At this season, the dry weather, the crops of maize and kaffir corn had been harvested, the land was being broken in preparation for the long rains, so that there were large areas of stubble and newly cleared land which were easier to examine for surface indications than the bush. The inhabitants were only too pleased to have work and pay without the necessity of leaving their Reserve to look for it, while from our point of view the natural fertility of the country made the feeding of the labour a simple matter. There was one drawback, a serious one for prospectors, in such homely and pleasant surroundings, namely, the necessity of obtaining from the owner of the land permission to dig a trench or even to drive in a post. Even if operations were begun in the middle of a dense patch of bush on the steep bank of some stream, in a place obviously useless for cultivation, before many hours had elapsed some native would turn up demanding compensation for the bush which had been cut down.

One could well understand their reluctance for having cultivated land defaced by trenches, but, by a strange perversity, the most promising place for opening a trench would inevitably prove to be the site of some hut or in the midst of a banana grove. To remove a few banana-trees, which could be replaced in eighteen months, was as sacrilegious an act as the cutting down of a whole avenue of immemorial oaks, and the value placed on them put even the prospective gold-mine to shame. In most places, either on cultivated or uncultivated land, the owners were reasonable enough; only too pleased, in fact, to be paid for allowing a trench to be dug and then filled in, for the filling in of trenches after they had served their purpose was obligatory. If the trench happened to cut a reef which justified further investigation, it would still be filled in, but a shaft, occupying perhaps only a space ten feet by twelve feet, could be sunk instead.

There were fixed rates of compensation for everything; so much for trenching, so much for the ground occupied by one's tent or hut, so much for the trees and grass used in building a hut. Money was asked and paid for putting in a peg or for making a six-inch hole with an earth-auger, no matter where, while the unlikeliest bit of land soon found an owner who was just about to start its cultivation. Thus encouraged, the natives became 'compensation-minded,' and found in us and other prospectors scouring their country a source of revenue that a Chicago racketeer might have envied.

After six weeks of strenuous work we had pegged and registered forty claims. Of the two operations, registration was the more difficult. Many forms had to be filled in and many maps drawn (all in triplicate) before being submitted to the Mining Office at Kakamega for inspection and approval. The passing and registration of these claims in less than three separate visits to the office was unusual, and rather suggested some oversight on the part of the inspector, for the details required were many and the scrutiny severe.

Since these excursions to the growing town of Kakamega added a little variation to life, and gave us an opportunity to collect our mail, they were not entirely unwelcome.

The post office for this mining population of one thousand was a tin shed ten feet square. It was understaffed, yet overcrowded by a staff consisting of an Indian babu and his native assistant, of whose qualifications for the post, except for a disarming grin, it would be rash to say anything. Add to this that many of the letters bore strange foreign names in the difficult spidery writing affected by the continental nations—whose owners had no English—and it will be readily understood that the scene when the mail arrived was more amusing for the onlooker than for the participant. Outside, sweltering in the sun, was a seething queue of angry miners; while inside, the babu, ankle deep in mail, sorted with slow, maddening, methodical deliberation, trampling underfoot halfpenny circulars and registered letters with calm indifference.

Having played an active part in this drama of the mail delivery or having got the worst of a wordy battle with the Commissioner of Mines, it was a relief to be able to turn to places in Kakamega where the tempo of life ran more smoothly—to a recently constructed hotel where, at immoderate expense, a much-needed restorative could be obtained. Emerging from the hotel, bemused but once again benevolent, there were several interesting things that one might see before returning home. It was but a step from the bar to the strategically placed stockbroker's office, resembling very much a hen-coop on wheels, where one gazed with solemn interest at the latest share prices displayed outside on a blackboard. Further down the very bumpy earth street were the many stores which had sprung up in this town of mushroom growth, where every mining tool imaginable could be bought, or at least priced. Here were cunningly constructed sluices for alluvial mining, small stamp batteries for crushing quartz, pumps, windlasses, and even crash helmets to safeguard the miner's skull when grovelling in the bowels of the earth. More important and exciting than anything else, however, were our periodic visits to the assayer's office, either taking in fresh samples or learning that our hopes of yesterday had again proved barren—a verdict which sent us home long-faced and wondering whether the fellow could find gold in a sovereign.

As pressure of work grew less we turned our attention to securing a better home. The approach of the rainy season necessitated more adequate protection than that afforded by a tent. Mosquitoes were troublesome at our present camp by the river; moreover, the tent had been so long in one position that rats and jiggers had become a plague.

The jiggers preferred me as a host rather than D., and before long I was having four or five extracted daily, or nightly, for the irritation is so intense that sleep is impossible until the offending insect has been removed. Natives are very quick at spotting them and taking them out, but they seem curiously indifferent about attending to their own feet, for it is not uncommon to see a boy minus a toe or two as a result of neglected jiggers. The rats had more affinity for D., so that he, too, had many disturbed nights. Under these afflictions I was eager to be gone, but D. was a keen fisherman who liked to spend his evenings ringing the changes fruitlessly with flies, spoons, meat, dough, and locusts, and he was loath to leave the river. There were plenty of fish there, but a stick of dynamite seemed to be the only lure they understood. However, it solaced D. greatly to thrash the water. There were no elephants here to chase, and the reef that we were chasing was proving even more elusive than our friends of the Gubba. I think we might have been camped by that river yet had not a rat contrived one night to get inside D.'s mosquito net. He and the rat were of one mind about getting out, but his anxiety to be first was fatal to the net, the bed, and almost the tent—everything, in fact, except the rat. We moved next morning.

Our new home was on high ground at the other end of our claims; too far from the river for D.'s peace of mind. Here, in the course of three or four weeks, we built a three-roomed mud and wattle house thatched with grass. Its size and elegance astonished the natives, who were now convinced that the lumps of barren quartz we were so assiduously collecting must be the source of our new wealth now made so unmistakably evident. The house finished, I made it my business to start a flower and vegetable garden, since it now seemed likely that there would be time to raise and eat a quick-growing crop like peas before we sold out for a few thousands and went elsewhere. Our hopes were still pitched pretty high, but we recognised that it was necessary to develop our holdings a little, and so provide something more tangible than hope before asking the prospective buyer to pay us a visit.

Another amenity was added by the discovery and opening up of a new route to the main road, a route which made it possible to keep the car on the same side of the river as ourselves. Hitherto, this had sat, forlorn and unhoused, on the far bank of the river, as if discarded by someone in a fit of pique, and, though a two-mile walk, followed by the removal of boots, socks, and trousers, to reach one's garage may at first amuse, it soon becomes a bore, and with the advent of the rains the river would become unfordable.

D.'s greed for claims was still unsatisfied. He argued that it was impossible to have too much of a good thing. I disagreed, partly on account of the cost of registration (£1 per claim), but also, and more particularly, because no one but ourselves had yet shown the slightest interest in this part of the country. This neglect puzzled me, for, although I might agree with D. that in enterprise and acumen we were in a class of our own, it did seem a little odd that of all the people scouring the country for claims not one had thought it worth while putting a peg in anywhere near us. We argued and debated our future course of action with the earnestness due to its importance, and, like the tribe of whom Gibbons writes, we took counsel together when drunk to give our resolutions fire and when sober to give them moderation. Finally, we pegged ten more claims and then devoted our dwindling resources to development work.

Having settled this momentous question, D. departed to his farm, leaving me to prove our claims. Only a dozen boys were employed, but, as there was work going on in five widely separated places, supervision, sampling, and further prospecting kept my days fully employed. In the evening I cultivated my garden.

As a result of five months' work we found and exposed five different quartz reefs, only one of which carried gold, and that a miserable two and a half pennyweights to the ton (which, of course, was not good enough). In large-scale mining such as on the Rand, a value of five pennyweights, or less with the present price of gold, is considered profitable, but, for a small reef, a value of ten pennyweights is the least that can be entertained. This bearing reef was a peculiar one, and our experience with it was typical of the disappointments which in gold-mining are the rule and not the exception. The 'floats' which were found on the surface near by gave a surprisingly rich 'colour' when panned. After digging many trenches in various places the reef was at last struck, and proved to be a good solid affair about three feet thick and lying almost vertically like a wall. Samples of rock were taken at different places, and on both faces, along the exposed portion, pounded up, mixed well together, and assayed, with the poor result stated.

It was, therefore, time to face facts; the glamour of mining was wearing thin, and the stick of our rocketlike hopes had almost come down to earth, but, before throwing our hand in, it was decided to sink a shaft alongside the bearing reef in the hope that it would 'improve at depth.' The hoary and oft-quoted adage that a reef is often richer lower down—so comforting and alluring a theory to the discoverer of a large but barren reef—must be responsible for many deep and abortive holes in the ground. Fortunately for us, we had not far to dig before finding a very convincing reason for stopping. The shaft was sunk close to the reef, and at a depth of forty feet I thought it would be a good plan to make a horizontal drive to see how the reef was getting on. We drove for ten feet, which should have been enough to cut it, but there was no vestige of reef, not even the odd lumps and the small 'stringers' which are usually found in the vicinity of a large body of quartz. To make sure, we drove for twenty feet clean through where it should have been, but it had already petered out.

From the safe distance of his farm D. would not acknowledge defeat; he seemed to think I had temporarily mislaid or overlooked the three-foot-thick wall as one might a collar-stud. But, backed by another disappointing assay, I was firm, for in this game it is fatally easy to allow hope to triumph over experience, and one lucky but unfair sample from a richer part of the reef is enough to start one sinking deeper again. Though there are many stories of men missing fortunes which another stroke of the pick or a foot deeper shaft would have revealed, less is heard of the fortunes which have been lost through not knowing when to stop. There was a provision in the prospecting regulations which, though not inserted for the express purpose, did something to insure against this tendency to go on trying till the last cent had been spent. Before a prospecting licence was granted, a deposit of £25 had to be made, so that when a man did reach the end of his tether there was always this amount in reserve to pay his debts and see him out of the field.

We had not reached that stage yet, and I thought it was time to notify D. that I for one had no intention of reaching it. In this he very unwillingly acquiesced, but he did not return for the celebration of the last sad rites, which took place only six months after the project had been born. The filling in of the shaft and the numerous trenches was depressingly like a burial, even though it were only our hopes that were being interred. He did come back later while I was still winding up our affairs (I was in no hurry to quit, having nowhere to go; also the vegetables were coming on nicely), and managed by eloquence and a brazen forehead to persuade our nearest neighbours, not unappropriately named the 'Golden Goose Syndicate,' to pay us £25 for the privilege of further investigating our claims. They were driven to this magnanimity by sheer desperation, because, although they had an area much larger than ours, they had not found even so much as a 'float' that gave any 'colour.' We could at least show them something better than that, and that we had lost nothing in the showing—indeed, the rich pans we found for them, and D.'s convincing eloquence, made me wonder why we were selling at all.

Before we left, the fever and excitement had died down, leaving in its place a healthier feeling of strong hopefulness. Like ourselves, most people began to realise that reef-chasing on this field was no game for the poor; for it was only here and there a man struck a rich, easily worked pocket and did well out of it. Big companies, able to take a longer view, had now entered the field, and, satisfied with the prospects, were quietly buying options on claims. The prices offered led one to suppose that they were actuated by pity rather than a desire to acquire something of value, but as a rule the seller had little development to show and was not in a position to wait.

No doubt the successful gold-digger must always be a gambler, with a philosophy of life resembling that of the Australian opal-gouger: 'Live in hope, if you die in despair.' Possibly a few years hence my friend D. and kindred spirits will shake their heads, cursing fate and pusillanimous partners, when they read of the riches found underlying the claims which they once had held and had abandoned.

CHAPTER XII

KILIMANJARO ALONE

For solitude sometimes is best society,
And short retirement urges sweet return.

—Milton

FEELING NOT MUCH SADDER and very little wiser after our experiences, we returned together to the Sotik, D. to his farm and myself for a few days' rest and relaxation, while deciding on my next move. During this visit a gymkhana took place in which, for my sins, I was given a ride in the big race. The distance was one and a half miles, and as we entered the straight a herd of oxen strayed on to the course. The rest of the field passed in safety, but I was not so fortunate. My mount, lying last and galloping full split, hit one broadside on, and I was catapulted over the horse's head. I slid along on my face several yards, 'biting the dust' in a very literal fashion—bit it to such a purpose, in fact, that most of my teeth were unshipped.

With a very sore mouth, and hardly able to talk intelligibly, I fled to Nairobi, and left again almost at once for Kilimanjaro. There were several reasons for this, chief among them being, perhaps, the temporary shortage of teeth and some diffidence about appearing in public, but also a desire for a return match with this mountain, for it will be remembered that in 1930 we did not accomplish all that we should have done.

At the risk of perhaps needless repetition, it is advisable to mention again that the summit of Kibo, which is the main peak of Kilimanjaro, consists of an ice-filled crater some 800 yards in diameter divided in the middle by a low ridge running east and west. The rim of the crater is the actual top of the mountain, the highest point on this long circular wall lying on the south side and named Kaiser Wilhelm Spitze. Between the point at which the crater wall is first reached and this highest point, a distance of perhaps 600 or 700 yards, are three other peaks, points, or bumps of varying heights, all slightly lower than Kaiser Wilhelm Spitze itself. These several points were always the cause of much heartburning.

In appearance they are all very similar, and in thick weather or soft snow the climber is quite happy to stop at the first, second, or third reached, on the false assumption that that is the summit. In 1930 we had to contend with both these handicaps, so, when the mist prevented us from seeing any point higher than the one on which we stood, we were satisfied with what we had done—the more so because we had not breath or energy for any more. Since that time a newly formed Mountain Club, with good intentions but with deplorable taste, has removed what little difficulty (and therefore fun) there was to be had by labelling each point with a small iron name-plate, so that the weary aspirant has no longer any adequate excuse for self-deception.

At each of these name-plates there is a receptacle of some kind for records, so that for the conscientious mountaineer on Kibo a card-case is a necessity. It was the omission to leave our full quota of cards in 1930 that I now wished to repair. As S. was not available, I had to go alone, and although solitary climbing is not in accordance with sound mountaineering practice, Kilimanjaro is, perhaps, a mountain where this vice can be indulged in with more safety than usual. There are no technical climbing difficulties apart from those consequent on the great altitude, while it is well provided with huts. A new one has been built at 16,000 feet, the jumping-off place for the summit, and to this it is possible to take a heavily laden caravan of porters. In 1930 we took a donkey there. All this extraneous assistance hardly gives the mountain a fair chance, so this time I decided to dispense with at least some of it and to carry what I wanted myself. I suppose, to be logical, I should have sternly avoided the huts, but I was content to follow the very sound maxim of the ancients: 'Nothing in excess.' With a companion it might have been different, for discomfort can be borne with greater equanimity if shared by others.

Leaving Nairobi by car, in August, I found the road less rough and the plains greener than when we drove this way in 1930. My first objective was a place called Namanga, about 100 miles from Nairobi, whither I had been commissioned to take a new driving pinion for the back axle of a car whose owner was stranded there. Namanga has usurped the place of Longido as a halting-place on the way to Tanganyika, for there is a comfortable rest-house there which is much patronised. One of the advertised attractions for visitors is a close view of a herd of elephants which haunts some neighbouring bush. For large parties it is advisable to reserve accommodation, and, since there is no mail or telegraph service to Namanga, this is done by means of the nightly broadcast from Nairobi wireless station. If the visitors desire to see elephants, this request is usually included, so that the message heard after the nine o'clock news may run something like this: 'Manager Namanga rest-house. Party of six arriving tomorrow. Elephants required.'

I got there about four o'clock and found my stranded motorist. He was on his way to the coast for a fortnight's holiday, but four days of it had already been passed here, so that even the elephants had begun to pall. He was all joy, like a prisoner who has been reprieved, when he heard I had something for him. I handed over the spare part amidst an embarrassing accompaniment of compliments and thanks for a very trivial service. I went in for a cup of tea while the castaway wrestled with his back axle, and, on coming out again, perceived at once that all was far from well. Curses and lamentations filled the air, and I was soon told with excusable heat and emphasis that the part I had brought did not fit the car. I was not to be blamed for that, but as 'the first bringer of unwelcome news hath but a losing office,' and as I could see that my presence at Namanga that night would be like an irritant in the wound, I pushed on. Driving slowly onwards in the darkness until about eight o'clock, I eventually came to some natives camped by the roadside round a large fire. Since I was to sleep out, one place was as good as another, so, pulling the car off the road, I got them to boil some water for tea and then curled up to sleep in the box-body of the car.

Next day I reached Marungu, putting up at the same little hotel where I had been previously received by the kind German host and his wife. The beautiful simplicity of my plan and its attendant advantages were now fully appreciated, for, instead of spending the remainder of the day haggling with greedy porters over wages, rations, clothes, packing and weighing loads, I had nothing to do but loaf about, inspect critically the local coffee shambas, and drink beer. In the morning, having packed a rucksack with sleeping-bag, warm clothing, and seven days' food, I told my astonished host to expect me when he saw me and walked off into the forest.

My load was quite heavy enough for me, weighing some 40 lbs.—a weight that did not include that of a tent which I had wanted to take in order to spend a night on the top. The weather was bad. A fine rain fell, while higher up the mountain was shrouded in mist. Showers of water dripped from every branch, so that it was not long before I reached the comparatively happy state of being unable to get any wetter. It is the long-drawn-out process of getting wet that is unpleasant, and when saturation point is reached one ceases to care. Approaching Bismarck Hut, one passes through grass glades, where the path was faintly marked and much confused by numerous elephant tracks. For ten panicky minutes I was astray and completely at a loss, and, in view of my earlier scorn for huts, it was astonishing how anxious I was to find one, how relieved when I did.

As I reached it in good time—at one o'clock—I had the whole afternoon to collect fuel and dry clothes. Next day was a repetition of the first—mist and rain—but once clear of the forest there was little difficulty in sticking to the path. This mounts by what the French guidebooks call *une pente insensible*, but at that height, carrying a heavy load, I was by no means insensible of it.

There was a sharp frost that night at Peters's Hut, giving promise of better things to come, and, soon after leaving the hut next morning, I passed out of the mist and cloud below and emerged into blazing sunshine under a cloudless blue sky. The height was 13,000 feet.

Approaching the 'saddle' at nearly 16,000 feet, I saw a herd of twenty-seven eland. These are the largest of all the antelopes; they weigh as much as 1000 lbs. and the meat is very tender and juicy. Both sexes are horned, those of a bull averaging twenty-five inches, and they stand five to six feet high at the shoulder. They are so gentle by nature that they can be domesticated, and in one instance at least have been trained for draught purposes. Butter made from eland's milk is said to be of exceptional quality. Their normal habitat is the open plains at heights of 5000 feet to 6000 feet, but so far as one could tell the eland up on the 'saddle' at 16,000 feet were in no way different, except for apparently shaggier hair. They seemed to be subsisting very happily on a diet of shale, and were very shy.

Looking at the two peaks of Kibo and Mawenzi and recalling our visit of 1930, I was amazed to see the very striking difference in conditions which now prevailed. The present year of 1933 had been an exceptionally dry one throughout East Africa, so that the snow on Kibo scarcely descended further than Leopard's Point, just below the lip of the crater. Mawenzi was completely bare of snow. The steep snow gully up which we had kicked steps was rust-red rock, with the result that neither as a climb nor as a peak did it look so attractive as when draped in snow and ice.

The local Mountain Club, which has marked Kibo's hoary head with tin insults, has done the mountain a further disservice by building a new hut a few hundred feet above the Hans Meyer Caves. It seemed to me that camping out for the sake of camping was neither useful nor beneficial, and, as there was a roof available, pointless. Backed by such specious reasoning, by the well-remembered draughtiness of the caves, and hoping to mortify the flesh next night by sleeping on the top, I condescended to make use of the hut. Near it there was another herd of eland, and if only the Mountain Club would domesticate these, and supply the hut with milk and butter, nothing would be wanting to the improvement of Kilimanjaro but a motor road.

The unusual absence of snow on the lower slopes made it difficult to find water. I had to search in nooks and crannies of the rocks above the caves before I could scrape together enough old snow for my wants. Next morning, carrying a light load consisting of sleeping-bag and two days' food, I started for the top before sunrise—at about half past five. In normal years the snow lies as low as 17,000 feet, but now I toiled up loose scree until Leopard's Point, just below the crater rim, was reached. Leopard's Point is a little rocky knoll on top of which lies the desiccated remains of a leopard. I have never heard any explanation of how it came to be there, but presumably it went up of its own volition. A similar curiosity is the buffalo skeleton high up on Kenya, but that lies at a place nearly 3000 feet lower than the leopard on Kibo.

It was delightful weather here, clear, sunny, windless. Below, at the 12,000 feet level, was a billowing sea of cloud which broke against the mountain, sending up wisps of mist like spray, which were in turn quickly dispersed by the sun. I seemed to be alone on an island detached from the world, floating in space on a sea of cloud.

The crater wall was gained at about 19,000 feet without any difficulty, under conditions much different from those of my first visit. The snow was hard and not even continuous, for in places it had melted away, leaving the bare rock exposed, while the whole of the crater, the rim and its several 'peaks,' lay clear and glistening in the vivid light. I looked down a short, easy snow-slope to the flat snow-covered floor of the crater, and across to the opposite wall half a mile away. Now begins the slow and arduous perambulation of the rim, passing over the sequence of 'bumps'—they are really little more—each honoured with the name of 'point.' In the order reached they are Gillman, Stella (our furthest in 1930), Hans Meyer, Kaiser Wilhelm Spitze (the true summit), and one beyond it called Furtwängler. Taken together, the names, with one exception, provide an awful example of what mountains have to suffer in the way of nomenclature.

I have not discovered who Gillman was; Hans Meyer, who was the first to climb the mountain, deserves to be remembered, but whether that can be said of the fourth name is open to doubt. Furtwängler, I am told, was the first to use skis on Kibo.

The earnest mountaineer sheds a card at each, and at Kaiser Wilhelm Spitze, which I reached at midday, there is a receptacle for records somewhat resembling, and almost as big as, a deed-box. In this are a miscellany of personal records, a Union Jack, and a Bible. Records can be found on all the points if the trouble to search for them in the snow is taken. There are few who would not take this trouble, for, however much one may despise the custom of leaving one's name on a mountain, it is at any rate one which furnishes an ever welcome excuse for a rest.

Furtwängler is about one hundred yards beyond the summit, and at first seemed higher, but a change of view-point showed it to be obviously lower. I sat there for some time, enjoying the sense of aloofness which the dense curtain of cloud below gave me, but the mist now began to prevail in its battle with the sun, which was presently hidden by a veil. No longer had it the power to disperse the upshooting jets torn from clouds as they broke against the mountain, and these, gradually coalescing, produced a slight but persistent fall of sleet.

Descending one or two hundred feet of snow and rock on the inner slope of the rim, I reached the crater floor and began casting about for a place in which to spend the night. A rather inadequately overhanging rock was soon found, and, having dumped my sack there, I walked across to the north side of the crater to inspect a secondary and very perfectly formed crater. At the top the diameter was about 400 yards across, at the bottom 200 yards. Sulphurous fumes rose from the lip, and pieces of sulphur lay about.

After taking photos and collecting some of the sulphur, I returned to the bivouac to turn in about 4.30, after a little food had been forced down. I was beginning to feel the effects of altitude, and suffered slightly from nausea and lassitude, but it was very noticeable that these symptoms were not nearly so well marked as in 1930, substantiating the well-known fact that acclimatisation is retained to a certain degree over long periods. In 1930 I was sick at 17,000 feet, sick most of the way up, and on top suffered from excessive willingness to sit down, whereas this time it was only after some hours on top (having also carried a load there) that I felt there was a remote possibility of losing my breakfast, but actually did not.

As soon as the sun sank behind the western wall, which it did quite early, and a thin wind began stirring, the deficiencies of my bivouac became apparent. I built a low stone wall to break the force of the wind, but wind is like water, and, though an imperfect barrier may check the ingress of some, that which enters spurts through with redoubled force. However, the night passed sufficiently well, half sleeping, half shivering, without complaint, for it would be unbecoming to criticise the hospitality of the mountain after sneering at that offered by man.

Dawn, nevertheless, was very welcome. I rose, cold and stiff, packed up, and crossed the crater floor in the direction of Leopard's Point. In places the snow in the crater had assumed a most curious formation, standing up in thin sheets like the leaves of a book lying open on its back. Each leaf was about six inches apart, and two feet high, and was too fragile to support the book. They had to be broken down before solid footing was reached.

This formation appears to have some affinity with the *neige pénitente*, or 'penitent snow,' of the Andes; so called from a supposed resemblance to cowled Penitent Friars. The name would have no sense if applied to the Kilimanjaro formation, but in the Andes, where it consists of fields of cones or pyramids of snow set close beside each other, slightly hooked at the top, and four or five feet in height, the name is more applicable. In his book *The Highest Andes*, Fitzgerald says the effect is produced by the combined action of sun and wind upon the frozen mass of snow-field, the crystalline parts, upon which the sun has little melting power, remaining erect in this strange fashion. I believe that no really satisfactory explanation for this phenomenon has yet been given, but it seems probable that since this formation is seen only in snow found within the tropics it may be due to the peculiar effects of a vertical, or almost vertical, sun. The great ice pinnacles found on some Himalayan glaciers is another interesting formation for which it is not easy to account.

Romping down the slope from Leopard's Point was a pleasant change, and, arriving at the top hut about eight, I had breakfast there before pushing on to Peters's, where the night was spent. Lunch next day was eaten at Marungu with mine host, who was with difficulty convinced of the fact that thirty hours ago I had been on the summit.

Hoping to reach Nairobi in the day, I made an early start, and, soon after leaving Marungu, passed my stranded motorist of Namanga. He was still on his way to the coast to enjoy the three remaining days of his fortnight's holiday.

I failed to reach Nairobi, and spent the night in the car in the middle of the Game Reserve. As I sat at dusk by my fire, listening to the mournful cry of a hyena, the rays of a sun, which for me had already set, picked out, high up in a darkening sky, Kibo's snowy dome.

CHAPTER XIII

A NEW WAY HOME

In all matters before beginning a diligent preparation
should be made.

—Cicero

MEDITATION AND SOLITUDE upon the top of Kilimanjaro had not clarified my thoughts as I had hoped, so that when I got back to Nairobi I was still undecided as to my next movement. The lure of gold was still very strong, and but for a certain happening I might have again responded to the call. A large tract of country bordering the north shores of Lake Victoria had been reserved for private prospecting—a welcome departure from the usual custom of granting sole prospecting rights over vast areas to companies. As yet, however, it had not been declared open, and no one was allowed to prospect there until it was. Meanwhile, the spending of a weekend duck-shooting near the lake had led to D. and I travelling by road across a large part of this new area, and on our return journey a large number of quartz samples had, by some strange chance, found their way into the car. But the wicked do not always flourish, and so it was with us, for every sample we tested proved to be barren.

That decided me. I concluded (wrongly, I now believe) that it was not worth while hanging about until this new area was opened, and made up my mind to go home for a time. Being in no particular hurry, this seemed the opportune moment for carrying out a scheme with which I had been toying for some time, namely, the finding of an alternative to the usual east-coast route to Europe. I have no great liking for steamer travel at any time, and I was heartily sick of this route, but the alternative had to be at least as cheap—cheaper if possible—a consideration that rather narrowed the field of choice. Journey by air was out of the question; travelling via the Sudan and the Sahara by car, though doubtless exciting, would also be expensive, and in any case I was not in love with motoring, even in a desert. This overland journey had at that time been done by several parties in cars, and it required not only money, but also the mechanical ability to cope with the breakdowns that would be certain to occur. Walking, on the other hand, was cheap, and was, moreover, a method by which I was certain of arriving somewhere, but would need more time than even I could afford, so I compromised finally on the humble but ubiquitous push-bike. Having thus simply settled the means of locomotion, the route and the ultimate destination had to conform. The sudd, swamp, and water of the Nile route gave little scope for cycling, and little knowledge of geography was needed to realise that if I meant to go home overland all the way, it entailed the crossing of the Sahara. That is all very well for cars and camels, but there are waterless stretches of three or four hundred miles which made the idea of riding a bicycle across it absurd, apart from the impossibility of riding at all in sand. So there remained the west coast, and to that I determined to go, and from there take ship. The precise point on the coast at which I would aim could be decided later, when I knew more about it.

It will be seen, then, that this plan of riding to the west coast was arrived at by a series of logical steps, based on the premise that I wanted to get home. In addition to many less complimentary reasons ascribed to it, one friend suggested that the real motive was the possibility of selling bicycles to advantage on the west coast; this I have less hesitation in mentioning because, unlike the other reasons, it implies a modicum of lucidity or normality. But in fact I had two very good reasons, namely, to get home and to see the country, for ever since gazing down upon the Congo forest from the top of Ruwenzori I had longed to travel through it. I have been at some pains to make my motives clear lest this proposed journey should appear to be in the same category as many projects whose only object is notoriety. Had notoriety been sought, I might have ridden the bicycle backwards, or at least have done the thing properly and started from Mombasa, on the east coast, with the back wheel in the Indian Ocean under a battery of cameras. I particularly wanted to avoid cycling in Kenya, first because the road through it was already so familiar that the idea of 'push-biking' along it gave me no pleasure at all; and secondly, because, as I myself was known there, the notice that my appearance would attract was very distasteful to me. It may seem strange that a man riding a bicycle should attract attention, but in tropical Africa a white man thus occupied is very conspicuous indeed, the more so if he carries a pack on his back, more kit on the handle-bars, and sleeps by the roadside at night under nothing more substantial than a mosquito net.

I decided, therefore, to start from Kampala, in Uganda, the furthest point west reached by the Uganda Railway, and on September 14th I boarded the Uganda Mail at Nairobi on my way to England, unencumbered except for a rucksack. The railway journey is interesting, embracing, as it does, an extraordinary variety of scenery—desert, bush, forest; native villages and European farms, mountain and plain, rivers and lakes. Perhaps the most striking feature of all is the deep, wide gash of the eastern arm of the Great Rift Valley, down into which the line drops and then crosses some forty miles west of Nairobi. It was of peculiar interest to me because ten days later, in the Belgian Congo, I was to cross the western arm.

In structure the two are alike—steep scarps containing a broad flat valley—and in both are found lakes and volcanoes. These two branches are parts of a single rift system which begins south of the Zambezi and extends northwards to the Sudan and Abyssinia, a distance of 2000 miles. North of Lake Nyasa the Rift divides, its two arms enclosing the great mass of Lake Victoria, which is the only East African lake that does not lie in the floor of one or other of the two Rift Valley branches. In the western arm are the lakes of Tanganyika, Kivu, Edward, and Albert; in the eastern, Natron, Naivasha, Elmenteita, Nakuru, Hannington, Baringo, and Rudolph. Some geologists go so far as to link up the African Rift with that of the Red Sea, and its extension northwards to the Dead Sea and the valley of the Jordan.

Until 1928 the Uganda Railway terminated at Kisumu, a port on the eastern extremity of the Kavirondo Gulf of Lake Victoria. A branch line was then built from Nakuru to the Uasin Gisha Plateau and the northern highlands of Kenya, being subsequently extended into Uganda as far as Kampala. This is now the terminus, and the northern branch has become the main line.

Before reaching Kampala the railway crosses the Nile by a bridge just below the Ripon Falls, where the river issues from the lake. Here is the little town of Jinja, with its remarkable hippo-infested golf-course,

the sight of which from the train brought back memories of our journey to Ruwenzori. Thirty-six hours after leaving Nairobi the train
landed me at Kampala, where I spent one day choosing a bicycle and
buying stores.

Kampala is the commercial capital of Uganda, twenty-five miles
from Entebbe, the official capital. It is the seat of the Kabaka (the
native king of Buganda), and is built, like Rome, upon seven hills,
which form the respective centres for business, the king and his parlia-
ment, the Church Missionary Society, the Roman Catholic Mission,
and the residential area.

The Baganda, the natives of the Buganda Province which gives its
name to the whole Protectorate, are probably the most advanced and
intelligent natives of East Africa. Few ornaments are worn, mutilation
of the features or cicatrisation is not practised, and the body is completely clothed, formerly in cloth made from bark, but now in cotton
sheeting, made up in the form of a long nightgown reaching to the
ankles. It is called a kanzu, and is no doubt a result of Arab influence.
Dressed in this, with a little white skull-cap, a native is far more becom-
ingly garbed than in the European dress which they increasingly affect.
They are skilful potters and weavers of mats, music means a great deal
to them, and an additional mark of culture is the attention they have
always paid to road-making—an interest very unusual among so-called
savage tribes. In fact, the Baganda are very different indeed from the
Masai, Lumbwa, Kikuyu, Kavirondo, and other East African tribes,
having little in common with them except their colour.

This traditional interest in road-making has been maintained
and encouraged by a happy combination of circumstances resulting
mainly from the system of administration in force at the present day—
the system which is known as 'indirect rule'; that is to say, as much of
their former power and responsibility as possible is left in the hands of
the native king and his chiefs. In the matter of roads this system works
in the following way to produce remarkable results. By an old-established native custom the peasants are obliged to work for so many
days a year on objects of public importance—roads, bridges, or rest-
houses—and nowadays the chiefs take a greatly increased interest in
seeing where and how this involuntary labour is spent, not only in the
public capacity of chief, but in the private capacity of a car-owner; for,

thanks to cotton growing, Mr Ford, and 'hire-purchase,' most of the chiefs own motor-cars.

Cotton is the most important product of Uganda, and on it the prosperity of the natives mainly depends. This prosperity is by no means constant, but, combined with the excellence of the roads, it has been sufficiently great in the past to have had a very stimulating effect upon the bicycle trade, as it is the ambition of every native to own one. Kampala is the centre of this trade—which brings me back to my own reason for being here.

For me, the purchase of a bicycle presented some little difficulty. As I had not ridden one since pre-War days, my knowledge of the 'points' of one of these machines was a little rusty. Complicating the issue still more was the fact that the trade in Kampala was in the hands of wily Indians, so that my simple purchase soon resolved itself into a struggle wherein I tried to avoid getting 'stuck' with something which had been lying in stock during the three years' depression, deteriorating rapidly in the equatorial climate. One of this fraternity was as plausible as a horse-coper, and, while telling me the age of the stock of his numerous competitors, showed with pride the date of manufacture stamped on his own. If the date was correct it meant that the bicycles had only left the factory a short month ago. Certainly it was possible they had been sent out by the unusual and expensive way of air mail, but a simpler explanation seemed to be that the man was a liar. That this was correct the sequel showed. Passing the same shop later in the day with a bicycle bought elsewhere, I went in to get some valve tubing. While measuring a piece, which I pocketed without examining, my friend expressed his sorrow that I had had the oldest bicycle in Kampala planted on me, and doubted its ability to carry me much further than the outskirts of the town. The bicycle I still have, but his precious valve tubing was perished when I bought it.

The bicycle finally purchased was an ordinary English make, costing £6. I might have had a Japanese one for £2, but I felt that here at any rate was a case where 'Buying British' was sound policy for more reasons than that of patriotism.

The question of spare parts gave me some anxious thought, as it was extremely unlikely that any would be obtainable after leaving Kampala. It occurred to me that unless I took a complete spare bike I might as well take nothing at all, so nothing it was, except for a couple of spare inner tubes. In the event, this attitude of faith and hope was rewarded, for in the course of a fairly rough 3000 miles no vital part either dropped off or broke. On returning home I mentioned this fact to the makers, hoping, in my simple way, that they would be so pleased with my unsolicited testimonial that they would give me a new bicycle. However, behaving with true British phlegm, they managed to contain their enthusiasm within due bounds, so that all I received was a kind little note expressing the pleasure it gave the firm to hear of what had been no doubt an agreeable and satisfactory journey.

I took the two inner tubes because I imagined—quite wrongly, as it happened—that punctures would be an everyday occurrence. I did find that inner tubes could be obtained at one or two places *en route*, but spare parts were not to be had.

My ideas about the route were vague. I could get no maps of the Congo or the country north and west of it; the only one I possessed was a small-scale map of the whole African continent torn out of the back of a magazine. I decided to make first for Stanleyville, in the heart of the Congo, thereafter steering for any port that could be reached between Accra in the north and Benguela in the south. This gave me a sufficiently wide target of about 1500 miles at which to aim, so that my plans had the very desirable quality of elasticity.

My luggage consisted of a rucksack containing 20 lbs. weight of food, spare shirt, shorts, camera, and other necessities, with a small roll of bedding made up of a light sleeping-bag, mosquito net, and ground-sheet carried on the handle-bars, bringing the total weight up to 30 lbs. An eiderdown sleeping-bag, out of place though it may seem on the equator, served the purpose well. At heights of 8000 and 9000 feet on the Uganda-Congo border I slept *in* it, and in the sweltering lowlands through which the greater part of my route lay I slept *on* it. A tent, though desirable, was too heavy to carry.

The small amount of food taken from Kampala was, of course, exhausted in a few days, and for the rest of a journey of more than two months I relied mainly on the country. What could be had natu- rally depended on the presence of natives and their standard of living, which was not extravagantly high. Bananas were the main stand-by, particularly a big, coarse variety which, when roasted in the ashes, was

Signpost on the Nairobi-Kisumu road

very excellent and satisfying. Two of these were enough to give one the sensation of having dined. In Uganda and parts of the Congo bananas are the staple food, and the natives are said to distinguish two hundred varieties. There are three main classes: the female banana, which is cut green, cooked and served mashed, or dried and made into flour; the male banana, which is used for beer-making; and lastly the sweet banana, which we know, eaten raw as a fruit or baked green. The leaves of the banana provide plates, wrappings for food, and umbrellas.

Other articles which sometimes appeared in my dietary were eggs, potatoes, and occasional fruit-oranges or pawpaw. The last is delightful, resembling a small marrow in shape and tasting like a cantaloupe melon. The flesh contains a ferment which is capable of digesting meat, while even the leaves wrapped round meat are said to make it more tender. With a drop of lemon-juice and some sugar it makes an even more delightful approach to breakfast than grapefruit, but unfortunately, like the mango, it is too perishable to export to Europe. On this vegetarian diet (I had nothing else) I kept pretty fit. True, I lost two stone in weight, but it must be remembered that cycling on the equator is rather heating. Before leaving, a boy offered to come with me as a servant. I told him he could, but as I was not going to buy him a bicycle he must run behind the whole way. He refused this generous offer, but I think he was quite capable of doing it. In Kampala they still tell the story of some native sports which were held there, of which the great event was a Marathon race. The runners, some fifty in number, were accompanied by several Europeans on bicycles to see fair play. After the lapse of a few hours they re-entered the stadium in a compact body, just as they had left it, all cheering and shouting. They thought it far more fun to stick together; they could see no sense in racing. As for the unhappy cyclists, it was several hours later when they straggled in in ones and twos, dead-beat to a man.

After a preliminary canter round Kampala in the evening to assure myself that I could still ride, I was up very early next morning in order to be clear of the town before anyone was about. I was still dreadfully afraid of being stared at, and, although my sensitiveness on this point soon wore off, had I known what I was to suffer in this respect later the trip would have been abandoned forthwith. At the last moment, aghast at the weight imposed upon the back wheel, I removed the roll of bedding from the carrier to the handle-bars, and so weighty was the impression my full rucksack made on me that I considered the tearing off and scrapping of such superfluities as gear-case, mudguards, and even bell. Fortunately I was in too much of a hurry to be off to put this foolishness into effect, so I mounted and pedalled slowly westwards out of the town on the first stage of my long journey.

CHAPTER XIV

THROUGH UGANDA

◆

Let the blow fall soon or late,
Let what will be o'er me.
Give the face of earth around,
And the road before me.

—R. L. STEVENSON

As the sun swung up over the horizon and began to play upon my back, where the weight of the rucksack was now making itself felt, I began to have misgivings about the effect upon myself of riding all day under a tropical sun and of the additional 30-lbs. weight upon the bicycle, and it was borne upon me that this first day would be a crucial one. But, as has already been said, the Uganda roads are good, so that at sundown that evening, after I had reeled off nearly 60 miles without any sign of imminent collapse on the part of the bicycle or of sunstroke on the part of myself, I regarded the remaining 2950 miles with less respect.

For the first two or three days the scenery was typical of Eastern Uganda: an endless succession of low conical hills clad in dense forest, unbroken except for scattered banana groves, while between the hills lay wide flat bottoms through which flowed sluggish streams whose water was concealed beneath vast swamps of papyrus grass. The road switchbacked amongst the hills and was carried across the swamps on long causeways. A rather bright and shiny green, common alike to the cultivated banana patches, the tropical jungle, and the swamps, coloured the whole landscape.

My choice of camp the first night on the swampy shore of Lake Victoria was not a happy one. It was close to the depot of a road gang, whose huts I thought could be used as cover if rain fell, but mosquitoes abounded, forcing me to seek the shelter of my net as soon as the sun went down at six o'clock. My evening meal was taken under its protection.

While in Uganda and the Eastern Congo, I made it a rule not to sleep in native huts or rest-houses. (The last are thatched mud and wattle huts put up and maintained by the local headman for the use of officials on tour and other travellers. With the advent of the motor-car and the consequent abolition of the old slow-moving porter safari, they are falling into disuse.) The reason for this self-denial was the prevalence in those parts of the fever tick (*ornitho-dorus moubata*), the carrier of spirillum or relapsing fever. This tick infests native huts, rest-houses, and old camping-grounds, and its bite may result in a fever even more unpleasant than malaria. As a compromise, I camped when possible near to huts or rest-houses, but only for cover in case of rain. Sickness induced either by tick bites or by chills was a mischance that I could ill afford and did not care to contemplate.

The natives were always horrified at my sleeping out, and it was not easy to make them understand my reasons for it. On two occasions in Uganda, I heard lions grunting at night, but there was little to fear from them, while there was a good deal to fear from the tick-infested huts. The headman of the village near which I camped usually insisted on lighting an enormous fire near me and providing a couple of men armed with spears to act as a bodyguard. What prowling perils they warded off I cannot tell, but they successfully warded off my sleep by their loud and ceaseless chatter. All natives are inveterate talkers; a taciturn African is a freak; the result, possibly, of illiteracy. Cattle, goats, and women—in that order—are the staple topics, while their conversational tone is a hearty roar.

It may be thought rash, even foolhardy, to travel thus unarmed, sleeping outside in a country abounding in dangerous game, but the lightest weapon that would be worth while carrying to stop a lion or an elephant would weigh at least 10 lbs., and long and expensive formalities would have had to be gone through in order to take a rifle into foreign colonies.

I think the risk run from big game is slight provided you leave it alone. Of course, if you hunt it you may have reason to agree with that Frenchman who wrote in a natural history book of some animal (I forget which), 'Cet animal est tres méchant, quand on l'attaque il se défend.'

There have been cases recorded of unprovoked assaults by rhino, elephant, or buffalo, but it is generally found that the animal had been shot at and wounded by someone else previously, and therefore bore a grudge against any human being.

A man-eating lion is less common than a man-eating tiger (tigers, of course, are not found in Africa), but in Uganda there are occasionally outbreaks of man-killing by lions, and in Kenya there is the historic case of the man-eaters of Tsavo. The incidents are related in a book called *The Man-eaters of Tsavo*. They occurred at Tsavo, between Mombasa and Nairobi, when the railway-line was being built. Some thousands of coolies from India were employed on the construction of the line (for in those happy days the African native, except for a few Swahili porters from the coast, did not know what work was), and for weeks on end their camp was terrorised by a number of lions, which killed and carried off one or more coolies almost every night. Many efforts were made to kill or drive away the marauders, whose raids were threatening to put a stop to the building of the line by frightening away all the labour. One of these attempts is worth relating.

Three Europeans sat up one night for the lions in a railway carriage, leaving the door open through which to shoot. They must have dozed, for the first thing they knew was that a lion was shut inside the carriage with them, the weight of his spring having rocked the carriage and slammed to the door behind him. The carriage was fitted for sleeping, with two berths below and two above. The lion then proceeded to stand on the chest of a man in the lower berth while he seized the man above and then jumped out through the opposite window with his victim in his mouth.

Stories of the railway and the game are the more amusing on account of the incongruity of the two, but the railway runs through over two hundred miles of country set apart as a Game Reserve, and more game is perhaps seen from the train than from anywhere else. In the early days, when the Colony was small and the atmosphere more happy-go-lucky, it was not difficult to persuade the driver to stop while the passengers killed a buck, or took part in a lion hunt.

Nowadays lions are rarely seen from the train, the majority of the so-called lions reported by excited travellers new to the country being merely inoffensive and smelly hyenas. On one famous occasion the train was charged by a rhino, and the attention of the railway authorities ought to be drawn to the fact that the train in question must have been grossly overcrowded, as twenty people at the very least claim to have been sitting in the actual carriage against which the rhino dashed himself. There is another good story of a telegram which was received at Nairobi from the heroic babu in charge of the telegraph office of some station down the line. It ran, 'Three lions on platform, station-master in water-tank, please wire instructions.'

Lions are a popular subject in the business of big-game photography for the cinema which enjoyed such a vogue recently, the reason being that lions are more easily photographed than any other game. By the simple expedient of providing free meals of buck or zebra daily, the lions of a district are soon attracted to the spot, and after a few weeks of that sort of treatment they become almost tame.

On the Serengeti Plains, a famous shooting-ground, some wag has put up a notice-board with the following warning: 'Notice to Sportsmen. Shout before you shoot; these lions are accustomed to be fed.'

More common than the lion and more feared by the natives is the leopard, for this bold and cunning beast is quite capable of raiding a hut for the sake of a sheep or goat. Dogs, too, are very frequently taken by leopards, but a man is very unlikely to be attacked unless the animal is wounded or cornered.

On the whole, I think I ran little risk in travelling so improvidently through the haunts of lions, leopards, elephant and buffalo, nor was I ever molested by any of these fierce beasts. My immunity was due no doubt to the common-sense attitude which on this occasion I adopted; similar to that of the Johannesburg Jew in the early days who, when his pals asked him why he never went lion-hunting, replied that he saw no reason to, because he hadn't lost any.

I was now three days out from Kampala, and approaching the district of Ankole in Western Uganda. To reach it I had traversed the populous cotton-growing districts of Mengo and Masaka, where the road was seldom without traffic of some sort—lorries taking cotton to Kampala, a few natives on bicycles, and hundreds on foot carrying their raw cotton to the local Indian trader who lived in a ramshackle tin shanty by the roadside. On leaving that country, and almost until the west coast was reached, I had the road pretty much to myself. Once or twice a week a lorry might be met, but I do not remember seeing more than two bicycles, and neither of those were in motion. The constant stream of natives met with during the first few days put a great strain on my politeness. I had little breath to waste on shouting the usual greeting of 'Jambo,' and, owing to my heavy load and lack of practice, too much punctiliousness in returning salutes by hand resulted in a sudden swoop across the road, followed by some paralysing moments while I strove to regain my balance and my dignity. The heat, too, was very great, in spite of an elevation of between 3000 and 4000 feet. I felt it more on these first few days in Uganda than at any other time, partly, I suppose, because I was not yet hardened.

In Ankole the country changes to open, rolling, grassy downs almost bare of trees. It is higher, and therefore cooler, than Eastern Uganda. The natives consist of a ruling race, the Hamitic Banyankole, who are all pastoralists, and an inferior Bantu strain who do the agricultural and menial work for their superiors. The cattle of Ankole, said to number nearly five million head, are remarkable for the enormous horns they carry. Forest or bush are conspicuously lacking, a fact which doubtless accounts for the absence of the tsetse fly, for broad belts of the surrounding wooded country are infested.

This open country was preferable to the bush, forest, and swamp through which I had passed, but it had its drawbacks. If there were no tsetse fly, there were plenty of the harmless but more annoying kinds, as is generally the way in a cattle country. Against this minor plague there was no protection, and short of dismounting I was completely at their mercy, for I was still insufficiently familiar with my mount and the queer distribution of weight to be able to ride with one hand while employing the other to swat flies.

Mbarara, 180 miles from Kampala, was reached on the third day. It is the capital of Ankole and the place of residence of the native king and his prime minister, or Katakiro, though I am ashamed to say that of more interest to me was the fact that there was some beer to be had. From a road engineer I managed to learn something about my route. At that time there were two roads from Uganda to the Congo, both passing to the north of the great barrier presented by the Ruwenzori range. One of these went to Butiaba and by boat across Lake Albert, and the other further north still, via Rejaf in the Sudan. Neither of these was any use to me now, as I was too far to the south, but I learnt that a motor road was being built to pass south of Ruwenzori between Lakes Edward and Kivu to link up with the Belgian road from Lake Kivu to Stanleyville. It was not yet complete, but I was told that by leaving it at Kabale, the last administrative post in Uganda, I could get into the Congo by following the old caravan track, which, though it would involve much pushing up and walking down, would take me through very interesting country.

I was now fairly amongst the Ankole highlands, whose main features are rolling downs, swamp-filled valleys, and very little cultivation; a vast grazing-ground for huge herds of long-horned cattle, and many head of antelope, zebra, and other game. At a place called Lutobo, I found a delightfully situated rest-house, perched, like most of its kind, on the highest available hill, up which I was not too proud to hire a slave to push the bicycle. It was well kept and clean, but for safety I slept on the short-cut grass lawn outside, where I was glad to use the inside of my sleeping-bag for the first time, the height being now over 6000 feet. The only food to be had was an enormous wooden bowl of milk, but had it been a month later I might have had strawberries and cream, for there was a vegetable garden in the compound with a large strawberry bed. As yet none were ripe.

Near Kabale the country became very broken, and the road wound about through steep shut-in valleys where I did as much walking as riding. Kabale is the administrative centre for the Kigezi district, in the extreme southwest corner of Uganda. The District Commissioner lives there, and, wishing to get some more information about the caravan track I proposed following, I went to consult him. There was a long uphill grind to reach the seat of authority, which was built on an eminence truly Olympian. Added to the toil was some nervousness about the reception I would receive at the hands of the Presence, for I must have looked, even at this early stage, uncommonly like a 'down and out.' But my reception was cordial, and the expenditure of so much energy amply repaid by the receipt of much useful information concerning the difficult country between Kabale and the Congo.

Before leaving the town I managed to obtain, in exchange for East African shillings, a few hundred Belgian francs. By this time it was midday, but I pushed on, and a mile from the town turned off the road according to instructions. I was at once faced with a three-mile hill of appalling steepness up which, I confess, I bribed a small boy to push the bicycle. The midday heat was blistering, and I felt it would require all my remaining energy to get myself and the rucksack to the top. The descent was steep, but led to a deliciously cool-looking lake called Bunyoni. I crept down this with both brakes jammed on hard.

The lake had to be crossed, and while negotiating for the charter of a dugout I found time for some food and a bathe. The water was surprisingly cold (far too cold for crocodiles), the altitude being over 6500 feet. Bunyoni is the largest of the lakes of the Ankole highlands, being fifteen miles in length. It is very narrow, dotted with many small islands, and lies in a cup whose sides are steep and heavily wooded.

The long hour's sail across the lake was a restful interlude which I spun out as long as possible by having yet another bathe before landing. My crew of three, who had to do the paddling, anxious to make the voyage as short as possible, pointed out several desirable harbours, but I was firm, insisting on being taken to the place advised by the District Commissioner, which was at the extreme end of one arm of the lake. A break in the reed fringe was our only port, and, having landed, one of the paddlers rather surprisingly volunteered to push the bicycle up another long steep hill to a rest-house called Behungi. This climb, long though it was, made very little impression on the high walls of the deep depression in which the lake lay. I could see the track making short zigzags up the steep sides, and, learning that there was worse country ahead, I engaged my volunteer for another bout of pushing on the morrow.

My rations here consisted only of another giant bowl of milk. I turned in alongside a large fire, for it was very cold, but about midnight a heavy drizzle drove me to the shelter of the *banda*, with all its dire possibilities of lurking fever ticks.

The boy and I set off next morning while it was yet dark. Walking was to be my portion for some time, so there was no immediate need of light. The hills surrounding the lake were over 8000 feet high, covered in their upper parts with dense bamboo forest, which was the home of numerous elephant and buffalo. Their spoor was everywhere, but we saw nothing of the animals themselves or of the human inhabitants of this jungle—a race called Bativa, savage, semi-pygmies, who are said to have practised cannibalism in the not distant past.

From the rim of the bowl, and looking towards the Congo, there was a prospect as rich in colour as it was wide in extent. Far below, shimmering in the heat, stretched a reddish-coloured plain of lava, studded with little crater lakes of an intense turquoise blue, and ringed about with mighty volcanic peaks. Of these the huge bulk of Mahavura filled the foreground, its flanks covered with thick scrub almost to the rocky summit. It is the third highest of this remarkable group of volcanic peaks known as the Mfumbiro volcanoes. The name Virunga is sometimes applied to them, but that is merely a local native name for a mountain. Karisimbi, 14,780 feet, is the highest; one of them, called Nino Gonga, 11,386 feet, lying nearer to Lake Kivu, is still active. The several peaks extend in a chain east and west across the thirty-mile floor of the Rift Valley, and form the divide between the Nile and Congo basins. The largest affluent of Lake Victoria, and therefore of the Victoria Nile, the Kagera River, rises on the east; northwards the drainage falls into Lake Edward, which is the source of the Semliki River and the White Nile; while southwards and to the west the drainage is into Lake Kivu, whence it flows into Lake Tanganyika and the Congo River system.

On the top I dismissed my follower; prematurely, as it happened, for the descent to the plain was as arduous as the ascent, as at times the bicycle had to be carried bodily. On the lava plain the going was indescribably bad. The track, which was studded with lumps of rough lava, traversed a sort of natural slag heap, winding amongst small craters and volcanic cones; twelve miles of agonised bumping over rasping lava before I reached the frontier post of the Belgian Congo. It was a 'post' in the literal sense of the word. There was nothing there (and I thanked heaven for it) but a wooden post, silent and uninquisitive, stuck upright in the ground—no customs official, no police, not even a human being.

It was exactly a week since I had left Kampala.

CHAPTER XV

LAKE KIVU TO STANLEYVILLE

Where are forests hot as fire,
Wide as England, tall as a spire.

—R. L. STEVENSON

I SAT THERE CONTEMPLATING what had been done and what remained to do, wondering whether my tyres were as badly frayed as my temper; and there, in a weak, unguarded moment, I was tempted and fell. My self-imposed rules for the journey allowed of no assistance in the way of lifts, and hitherto my firmness of mind had not been severely tested. If, after leaving Mengo, I met more than one lorry every other day the road seemed congested. But now, while I was ruefully examining my tyres, the devil appeared in the guise of an Indian lorry-driver bound for Lake Kivu. He at once offered me a lift. Concern for my tyres silenced the haughty refusal hovering on my lips, and instead I asked him how far the horrible surface continued. On being told nearly to Ruchuru, the first Belgian post twenty miles away, I accepted his offer without more ado. It was flagrant cheating, but it is the only instance to be recorded, and I excused it on the grounds that it was necessary to save the tyres. It was a rougher ride in the lorry than it would have been on the bike, so that I was not sorry to dismount when we reached the Lake Kivu-Stanleyville road, two miles short of Ruchuru. I ought now to have turned north for Stanleyville, but as Lake Kivu, which I was anxious to see, was only fifty miles away, I turned south. We had got clear of the lava plain, and for a brief space I was once more in a country where man could live and cultivate. Near by Ruchuru there were several European coffee plantations whose appearance was the more startling following so hard upon the arid waste of lava over which I had come.

I stopped that night half-way between Ruchuru and the lake, at a Mission run by the White Fathers, where I was very hospitably received. It lay at the foot of one of the volcanoes, Mikeno (14,385 feet), a very striking peak whose summit consisted of a curved rocky fang. There was no vestige of a crater, as it had apparently been eroded away. Away in the south-west a lurid glow in the sky marked the activity of Nino Gonga—a fittingly baleful beacon to light such a desolate landscape.

The run from here to Kisenyi, on the lake-shore, was a well-balanced mixture of pain and pleasure. At first I regretted heartily the curiosity which had involved me in a hard grind in white lava dust along a road which wound amongst a chaos of lava boulders where dreary-looking trees and bushes struggled for existence. There were no huts, no villages, no water, no life. It is a fantastic country—part of what the Belgians call the Albert National Park. This is a big tract which has been set aside as a Game Reserve, where it is hoped that the fast-vanishing African gorilla, which, appropriately enough, haunts the wooded slopes of the volcanoes, may now have a chance to survive.

Near Lake Kivu there is a swift transition from desert to fertility. Lava boulders give place to a rich soil of volcanic ash which supports a dense population made up of natives called Wahuta. The womenfolk of these people outdo the Lumbwa, Masai, or Kikuyu women in the amount of wire which they coil about their ankles. The weight carried must amount to several pounds per leg, producing an appearance suggestive of elephantiasis.

The surface of the road also changed for the better, the low watershed had been crossed, and I freewheeled for nearly ten miles down to Kisenyi and the lake. The little port of Kisenyi, where I stopped the night, contained a white population of about a dozen, mostly Greeks. In Kenya and Uganda the Indian storekeeper is ubiquitous, but in the Congo his place is taken by the Greek. These two races seem able to thrive where the Englishman or the Belgian would starve. Possibly the secret lies in what it would be polite to call simple living, and in making full use of the natural resources of the country. This last point was well exemplified by my Greek host. I had put up at a little place kept by one of these Greeks which was styled rather grandiloquently The Lido—a name to which it had some claim, because the white sandy beach was not fifty yards away. My attention was drawn to this when I asked my Greek friend if I could get a bath. He looked at me as though I had made a joke in rather doubtful taste, and pointed out, quite rightly, that there was a perfectly good lake just outside his door!

When I came to act on this hint I was surprised to find that Kisenyi was as careful to observe the proprieties as Margate, so that I was compelled to borrow a bright red horror from my host and thus spoil an otherwise perfect bathe. The firm, clean, sandy beach shelved steeply into cool, limpid water, and but for the wretched entangling garment that bathe would have been hard to beat. Even so, it ranks high in my list of classic bathes, for the life-giving water closed over my head to drown the fatigues and sweeten the memories of the last ten days.

Lake Kivu was discovered in 1894 by Count Gotzen. It is 5000 feet above the sea, and in depth second only to Lake Tanganyika, which is the deepest of all the African lakes. Its green, fertile shores rise in places to 10,000 feet, wooded islands lend their beauty to its calm blue surface, its waters abound in fish, while hippos and crocodiles are entirely absent. It is considered by some to be the most beautiful of the African lakes; indeed, the Kisenyi bay has been compared to the Bay of Naples, but in my opinion it lacks the charm and the colour of the Kenya lakes, Naivasha, Nakuru, or Elmenteita.

I was now faced with the long stretch of 650 miles to Stanleyville. In a direct line, the town is only about 300 miles north-west of Kivu, but the road leads north, passing west of Lake Edward, Ruwenzori, and the south end of Lake Albert, reaching to Irumu before it at last turns west and heads for Stanleyville. While retracing my steps to Ruchuru, and for a day's journey beyond that place, I was riding along the trough of the western Rift Valley.

At Ruchuru, a small administrative post, the road takes a bend to the west, crossing the floor of the Rift to its western wall, which is formed here by the Kabasha escarpment. After leaving Ruchuru, cultivation ceased, and I rode through uninhabited country of open grassy plains on which herds of topi roamed. Wherever there was water the long grass was trampled into lanes with the tracks of hippo.

Not knowing for where the road was heading, and having no map, I was surprised and disquieted by this westerly bend. I had expected it to follow the valley, but on this new alignment it was with inexorable perversity making for a long range of high hills instead of running parallel to them as before. Towards evening I came to a few huts, which were the first habitations I had seen since leaving Ruchuru, so that when I perceived that the road meant to climb those high hills I decided to defer that pleasure and to camp.

I found that I was at the establishment of a native game warden and his underlings, for the country through which I had been travelling was another part of the Albert National Park. Approaching the huts, I had myself seen the freshly broken branch of a tree denoting the presence of elephant, and the natives now assured me that both these and lions were plentiful. The game warden urged me to share his hut, but, mindful still of the spirillum ticks, I preferred the dangers without to those within. In the end I tried both. Quite early in the night heavy rain drove me into the hut, and then, later on, by flooding the floor, drove me out again. I endured lying on the floor in a pool until three in the morning, when, the rain having stopped, I had some food and started pushing the bike up the escarpment in the dark, lions or no lions. Some light would have been agreeable, but it was by no means necessary, for I knew that the wet and heavy road surface with the formidable climb would prevent any riding for some time. Dawn came at six to find me still pushing, and it was after nine before the climbing of the first step of the escarpment enabled me to start pedalling again. When it was light enough to see, I found that I was on a well-made road zigzagging backwards and forwards up the rocky escarpment. This road up the 8000-feet Kabasha escarpment is a remarkable piece of engineering. It climbs nearly 4000 feet in less than twenty miles with a gradient of nowhere more than one in twenty.

The bleak uplands on top of the escarpment were sparsely inhabited. The few natives I did meet either fled at sight or crouched behind a bush—evidently a being on two wheels was to them something in the nature of a sign and a portent. Late the same evening I came to the first Belgian rest-house—what they call a *gîte d'étape*—but, still playing for safety, I slept outside by a roaring fire. It had been a gruelling fifteen-hour day, with fifty miles made good, twenty miles of it on foot.

If the spirillum tick is susceptible to cold, I should have been safe enough in the *banda*. Judging by the high altitude vegetation such as bamboo and bracken which flourished there, I estimated the height at 8000 feet. The native crops were potatoes and wimbe, the altitude being too high for maize or bananas.

Every road must go downhill sometimes, and next morning I had twenty-five miles of coasting. I passed a signboard which said forty-seven miles to Lubero, and, though I had no notion what Lubero was, I was cheered by this mute guide. There is a charm, rarely attainable in these ordered days, of travelling blindly, in profound ignorance of the country ahead, but it was comforting to know that one was on the way to somewhere. Little help could be got from the natives. Most of them knew nothing of the country outside their immediate neighbourhood, and no amount of interrogation could instruct me how far it was to any place beyond the next village, or where to make for to spend the night.

Lubero proved to be the centre of a thickly populated district. The natives were engaged mainly in growing potatoes of the European variety, which I was told were sent by road to Stanleyville and thence as far as Leopoldville, near the Congo mouth.

Pushing on through pleasant, healthy, fertile country, I stopped the night with a young American missionary from Texas. He had chosen a difficult place for his activities, having to contend not only with the heathen, but also the Roman Catholics, whose missions greatly preponderate in those parts. Every village almost had its church, in the shape of a grass hut surmounted by a cross, while every child seemed to bear a crucifix round its neck. It was a pleasant enough country in which to work. It was comparatively cool, free from fever, and capable of growing most kinds of European fruits and vegetables, many of which appeared at our meal that night. Being an American—a Southerner at that—and a man who had been living alone for some time, my host had a good deal of pent-up conversational steam to blow off. He was commendably frank about the local natives, and had not allowed enthusiasm for his mission to blind him to their faults. They were the Bananda, a poor, timid, undersized race, who, like the Wakamba of Kenya, had the custom of filing their teeth to a point. This custom, which makes a normally ugly face look ten times worse, is supposed to denote cannibal tendencies. Why it should is not quite clear to me, because no human flesh, not even a cyclist's, could possibly call for sharper teeth to chew than African chicken or goat. The nearest approach to human flesh that I have sampled is monkey, and that is not in the least tough.

Wayside scene: A war veteran mends the author's shirt

Wayside scene: Mosquito net and bicycle in front of a hut

The end of these cool, healthy uplands was now in sight, and next day, from the edge of another escarpment, I beheld, far below me, a smooth expanse of dark olive green stretching away into the distance, flat and unbroken, like the sea. It was the Congo forest, reaching westwards to the sea and extending to four degrees north and south of the equatorial line. That afternoon I entered what was to be my environment for the next fortnight. Within this tract of low-lying virgin forest, terrifying in its silent immensity, the atmosphere is that of a hothouse, sapping the energy of both mind and body. The only road crossing this sea of vegetation in which I was now submerged stretches endlessly before one like a thin red band at the bottom of a canyon of living greenery. The dark wall of foliage towers up on either hand for nearly 200 feet, to arch and almost meet overhead, as if to reclaim for the forest the pitiful strip that man has wrested from it.

As I watched the narrow red ribbon of road unwind slowly in front of my wheel, I felt as though I had been doomed to ride endlessly along the bottom of some enormous trench out of which it was impossible to climb.

The only break in the oppressive monotony were the villages, the huts of a road gang, and the rivers. The villages and the *cantonniers*, as the huts of the road gangs are called, are merely two single lines of huts spread along either side of the road. At the villages there is also a narrow strip of cultivation, perhaps thirty yards deep, overshadowed at the back by the dark wall of the forest, appearing thus envious at yielding even that insignificant patch to man, its enemy.

This is 'ribbon development' *in excelsis*. Everything centres on the road. Away from it is nothing human, except here, in the part called the Ituri Forest, a few pygmies, who live by hunting and who come into the villages to barter skins and meat for maize and bananas.

A very short stature of four feet or less, broad and flattened nose, prognathous chin, long arms and short legs, are the characteristics of these curious people. But, however inferior physically they may be, they are more mentally alive than the average negro. On the other hand, they live in the most primitive manner possible, in huts little better than the nests which gorillas make for themselves, and they are entirely ignorant of agriculture or of any industry but hunting. Though living a life similar to the Wanderobo of the Kenya forests, the Congo pygmies differ from them very notably in that they are by no means shy of other natives or Europeans, and will come readily into the villages for purposes of barter.

This part of the Congo forest called the Ituri is also the home of that strange animal the okapi, whose existence was first made known by the skins brought in by pygmies. It is allied to the giraffe—its forearms and thighs are striped like a zebra's. The horns, which are found only on the male, are covered with skin except on the tips.

The roadside population, which must comprise practically the whole, is complementary to the road; without the one there could not be the other. As the road was made, so the road-makers settled or were planted alongside—the only possible arrangement both for administration and trade in a country so inhibitive to movement. In the Congo, near towns or favoured areas, this 'ribbon development' had produced a long, continuous strip of life and activity, which in this primitive community has all the material advantages and none of the aesthetic drawbacks which a like development has at home. The huts may be dark, dirty, and, according to Western standards, only fit to be burnt, but darkness is rather pleasant in a country of blinding sunlight, the dirt is more apparent than real, and they are at least habitations adapted to the owners and their environment. The dignity of the Congo forest and the 'poor but honest' simplicity of its villages have not yet been menaced by bungaloid growths, corrugated iron, petrol pumps, and kiosks.

The villages, occurring every ten or fifteen miles, and rivers, form welcome breaks in the deadly monotony of the forest. Under the canopy of the forest, a network of rivers, great and small, which are at once a means of, and a barrier to, communication—tributaries of the mighty Congo—flow sluggishly between low banks, through valleys which are almost imperceptible, so uniformly flat is the surrounding country.

The first of the big rivers (and there were many), to which I came was also called the Ituri. It was reached at the end of a long day in country which for the last twenty miles had appeared to be uninhabited. The reason for the absence of villages, which I only discovered later, was that this tract was infested with elephants. No indication was given that I was approaching a large river. There was no warning descent; the road merely came to an end, terminating with the forest, on the brink of a quarter of a mile stretch of muddy, slow-moving water. At first I was at a loss how to cross, until I spotted a wire hawser spanning the river and on the far side a number of canoes. This first ferry was typical of many by which I crossed on the Kivu-Stanleyville road. It consisted of half a dozen dugout canoes supporting a rough plank platform big enough to hold a lorry. This contraption was attached to the wire cable by a pulley wheel, and, once it had been poled out into the stream by the crew, the force of the current, striking it at an angle, was sufficient to take it across.

By dint of shouting I got the ponderous affair manned and brought slowly across for its disproportionate freight. It seemed rather like chartering the Queen Mary to take one across the Channel. I learnt later that single canoes were provided for the conveyance of travellers on foot and idiots on bicycles. They were a good deal quicker than the ferry, and native passengers were carried free. The charge for the ferry made to lorries varied with the size of the river from three francs to ten.

I put up my net close to the huts of the ferrymen and was soon sound asleep. Much to my disgust—for I was very tired—I was presently awakened by the lights and hooting of a lorry. In England we are slowly being educated to accept the nightly roar of traffic as one of the amenities of civilisation, but it seemed a bit hard to suffer in the same way in the depths of the Congo. Anyhow, I am pretty sure it was after the legal hour for blowing a horn. My thoughts and imprecations on the menace of an advancing civilisation, capable already of disturbing the peace of an African night, were trite but malevolent, but I might have remembered that, had there been no such things as petrol engines, there would have been no road through the Congo. No animal transport, except perhaps elephant, could work there. In the end civilisation had the last and best laugh, for long before dawn I was again roused with a start from a deep sleep, to hear pandemonium raging on the far side of the river. A herd of elephants had come down to drink, and the squealing, trumpeting, and crashing of branches made further sleep impossible.

Reverting for a moment to transport, it is interesting to note that the Belgians have established an elephant farm and have taken in hand, with some success, the training of African elephants for draught purposes. Hannibal was the last to use the African elephant, which, unlike the Indian elephant, was thought to be too intractable to submit to harness until the Belgians, 2000 years later, once again demonstrated the contrary.

In 1929 the herd under training numbered about seventy, while some thirty had already been sold for agricultural purposes. Two are said to be able to draw a load of four tons fifteen miles, or plough an acre of land in a day. I remember one morning in the Congo spotting an elephant advancing down the road towards me. I was rather astonished, though there was no particular reason why an elephant should not come out of the forest to walk on the road, but I hastily prepared to waive any right of way. It was not until he got nearer that I saw he was trundling a cart behind him. I felt he was in more need of sympathy than his fellows who had fallen to a bullet.

In spite of a chill white mist hanging over the river early next morning, and the evil colour of the water, I was sorely tempted to bathe. But I refrained now, as I did until the Atlantic was reached, on account of the risk of acquiring some disease. The bilharzia parasite, producing an almost uniformly fatal disease, breeds in the many low-lying rivers in the tropics. Even walking about in bare feet provides an excellent opportunity of picking up hook-worm. Denying myself bathing and being unable to drink any but boiled water were severe deprivations for a man taking violent exercise in the atmosphere of a Turkish bath.

I was now well to the north of the Ruwenzori range, and almost level with Lake Albert, both of which, of course, were lying well to the east of my line. Before reaching Irumu the Stanleyville road branched off, but I was not sufficiently interested to push on to see this considerable town, which is the headquarters of the Kilo district, a rich gold-mining area.

Mambasa, a small administrative post, I also passed without stopping, although there was a *gîte d'étape*. I managed, however, to buy, or rather beg, a loaf of bread, which was a very infrequent luxury, for it was only obtainable in places where there were Europeans, who, naturally, were not often willing to part with bread made for their own use. In Kenya, whether on the farm or on safari, I never had any difficulty in getting a boy to turn out good bread; his yeast was made from sugar and a potato in a bottle which was always exploding, while his oven consisted of an empty four-gallon petrol tin.

If I could, I avoided stopping at the rest-house of these administrative posts, where there were generally one or two European officials or traders. I found it was much easier to have one's simple wants in the way of food, wood, and water supplied at a village, or even at a *cantonnier*. Sometimes one had occasion to regret this preference, as, for instance, the night on which I scorned the attractions of Mambasa. Having ridden on till almost dark and failed to find a village, I had to 'doss' down near one of these *cantonniers*. As soon as I turned in a *ngoma*, or dance, with drum accompaniment began just outside my mosquito net. In spite of my protests, it was kept up with maddening persistence and repetition until after midnight. I was chagrined to learn that it was not in honour of my arrival, but was merely an anticipatory celebration of payday, which was due the following day. I could not help cherishing a hope that some of them, especially the band, might be disappointed.

The question of finding a billet for the night or a place for the midday halt was ever a chancy one. In spite of the height of the trees which bordered the road—great 150-feet giants of mahogany, palisander, and cotton-trees, which overtopped a lower stratum of palms, tree ferns, and wild bananas, entwined and bound together with creepers—the midday sun beat through unmercifully. I used to start at the first faint streak of light just as soon as there was enough of the road visible to ride, and carry on until midday, when I had a two hours' halt before going on again until the sun went down at six o'clock. Even for the midday halt a village was better than the shade of the forest, because there one could get a fire to boil water without the trouble of making one, and pass the time of day with the natives.

I soon became adept at rapidly summing up the possibilities of any village; what the chances were of finding bananas, eggs, or fruit. But appearances, however promising, were usually deceptive. The bananas would be unripe, or possibly only of the cooking variety, the eggs would be too ripe, and the fruit-trees barren. Some of the villages seemed to have been provided with a few orange, lemon, or pawpaw trees by a paternal Government, but the treatment these received was a good example of the weakness of collective ownership. None of the trees was cared for, and the natural desire of each man to forestall his neighbour commonly resulted in any fruit that might form being picked before it was ripe.

On deciding to halt, the first thing I did was to call out for a chair, and it was a source of continual surprise to me to find that most villages in the Congo could produce a home-made chair, sometimes even a table. The chair was usually modelled in the style of a deck-chair, with a skin for the seat, and in it the owner seemed to spend more time than exponents of the gospel of hard work would approve. In Kenya a native would despise such a thing: not that he believes in hard work—far from it—but that he would be far more comfortable squatting on his hams, that agonising posture which a native seems able to assume and enjoy for an indefinite period.

These Congo natives were certainly far more advanced than those of East Africa, no doubt because they have been for a longer period in contact with Europeans. Instead of the primitive bee-skep-shaped, windowless huts common to East Africa, whose single aperture can only be entered on all fours, the huts along this Congo road are rectangular. They have windows which can be closed with shutters, doorways which can be entered without stooping, and a veranda in front where the owner lolls at ease in his deck-chair while he encourages his womenfolk to get on with the work. Roofing is always a difficulty, as there is no grass in the forest, and I was consulted by a missionary I met on the road as to how he could roof his house. It seemed strange to me to be in Africa and to be without grass—Africa's almost never-failing roofing material. All I could devise was to try growing some long-strawed wheat. The natives overcome the difficulty by using a particular kind of broad leaf cunningly pinned or laced together. It is satisfactory, but does not last long. The thatch is prepared on the ground in foot-wide strips of the length of the roof, the whole strip being then lifted bodily into position. The absence of grass is, of course, responsible for an absence of cattle. Goats and chickens are common, while, in many villages, lean razor-backed pigs, looking more like hyenas than pigs, can be seen.

When I had been accommodated with a chair and when I had bought whatever was going in the way of food—bananas, sweet pota-toes, or eggs—a fire would be brought from the nearest hut and what simple cooking there might be I attended to myself. Unless a native has had a lengthy training, food has little association in his mind with cleanliness, while, in addition, he can be counted upon to bungle the simplest job such as making tea or boiling an egg. It is possible to train natives into very good cooks and servants, but the task is often a heart-breaking one, requiring more time and patience than a man living alone on a farm can devote to it. When the trouble is taken, it often happens that the boy leaves for another job just when he has learnt how one likes things done.

On the principle of 'what the eye doesn't see the heart doesn't grieve for,' I would advise a man living alone on a farm to avoid his kitchen, or the grass hut which answers to that name. He might find, as I did, the cook or one of his friends combing his woolly, ghee-dressed hair with one of the best forks, or straining the soup or the coffee through a sock. When I remonstrated mildly with the cook about the last, he was quite hurt. My fuss he thought unnecessary, because, as he pointed out, indignantly but correctly, he was using not one of my clean socks, but only an old, dirty one.

On my leaving a village in the morning the present of a few cents to the headman, and to those who had brought wood and water or loaned me a chair, made everybody happy. Throughout the Congo they were hospitable and friendly, in spite of my poverty-stricken appear-ance and singular mode of travel, for, in tropical Africa, as in India, there is a tendency amongst natives to despise a white man who does any work with his hands, or walks instead of riding in a car. A smatter-ing of education seems to accentuate this tendency, so that the victims of the educational system in vogue begin to look on physical effort as not only beneath a white man's dignity, but beneath their own.

While more than 200 miles from Stanleyville I got my first puncture, and, as it occurred at the hottest time of the day, it was impossible to make a patch stick. During my struggles the rubber of the pump connection, which was slightly perished, fused solid in the heat, rendering the pump useless—a calamity which produced visions of pushing the bike for 200 miles to Stanleyville before finding another pump. However, my luck was in, for after walking only five miles I came to a big village of about four hundred inhabitants, all Mohammedans. It was a sort of Mohammedan oasis in a wilderness of pagans and semi-Christians, ruled over by a man who called himself an Arab, a descendant probably of Arab slavers. His name was Saili bin Salim (on his head be peace). He was very hospitable. He put a newly built hut at my disposal and caused some of his men to rig up a bed of sticks and branches inside. This was a timely act, because no sooner had I arrived than a most violent storm began. It continued most of the night, and was accompanied by terrific thunder and lightning, wind and torrential rain.

Strangely enough, there was a bicycle in this village, and the owner of it, learning that a fellow-cyclist had arrived, brought it along next morning to compare notes. More surprising still was the fact that there was also a pump; less surprising, and more in accord with natural laws, was the fact that it did not work. I could not make out his standing. He may have been cyclist by appointment to the local sultan or merely his bicycle-slave, but he was certainly equal to his job. He showed me a trick which I might have known myself, one which made me independent of pump connections. This was to apply the business end of the pump directly to the valve, over which was placed a piece of wet rag. Pumping was a slow business, but the trick worked and kept my tyres hard, but at Stanleyville I bought another pump connection.

The fierce rain of the night had made the surface so 'holding' that only walking was possible until after 7 a.m. Even then I had constantly to stop to clear the wheels of mud before they would turn round. A fierce sun soon dried the surface, enabling me to reach that afternoon the junction of the road which comes in from Rejaf in the Sudan. Pushing on, I stopped for the night at Avakubi, a small post on the winding and twisting Ituri River which had again to be crossed. It was now much wider, and the ferry journey across took half an hour.

There was a solitary trader with a native wife here, off whom I borrowed a loaf of bread before repairing to the rest-house. The trouble with these places is that they are always bare of furniture, compelling one to sleep on a brick or brick-hard mud floor. By sending out one could sometimes collect a chair—less frequently, a bed, the latter being either of split bamboo, which makes hard lying, or of rope, which is soft but dirty.

The road between Avakubi and Stanleyville was of much older construction. The villages were more numerous than heretofore; more land had been won from the forest, and some rice was grown.

My next billet was in a fly-ridden village where I had made for me, in the open, a rather elaborate bedstead of sticks, with a thick mattress of banana leaves to soften its asperities. I looked forward to a good night on this, but it was not to be. Soon after dark a thunderstorm blew up, so that I had to forsake my comfortable couch for the refuge of a hut. The loss of the bed was no great matter, but it was difficult to rig up my mosquito net in the hut in darkness. This was one of the few places since leaving Uganda where mosquitoes were troublesome: even when I turned out just before 4 a.m. to light the fire they were still numerous and very vicious.

Now that Stanleyville was near I became absurdly impatient to reach it. It marked a definite stage on my journey, and it was there I hoped to resolve my anxieties as to whether it was possible to reach the coast by road. This impatience manifested itself by very early starts, short midday halts, and late finishes, which combined to give me some very restless nights. It is about this stage that there appears in my diary a severe diatribe on the wretched camps I was enduring—a reflection that was made more pointed when I remembered the delightful camps we sometimes enjoyed on our shooting safaris. 'Tied to the road with a bike,' I wrote, 'there is no choice, but what rotten camps I have had; differing only in degrees of badness, but having the worst feature in common—a gaping crowd which cannot be escaped and which is wearing me out.' In certain places the crowds became almost unendurable, giving me a faint notion of what men like Mungo Park in West Africa, or, later on, Joseph Thomson in East Africa, had had to endure for months, or even years. Those men travelled alone, without an army of porters and armed guards, relying for permission to travel—nay, even for life itself—upon the goodwill of the natives, a goodwill which sometimes could only be bought by the cheerful suffering of all kinds of familiarities and indignities—with never a moment's privacy.

After twenty-one days on the road I rode into Stanleyville on a blistering hot afternoon, endeavouring to assume an air of nonchalance, as though riding in from close by for an afternoon's shopping. The effect was rather spoilt when I fell off in the main street with the bicycle on top of me. I was very tired.

CHAPTER XVI

NORTH TO BANGUI

Turn, turn my wheel! Turn round and round,
Without a pause, without a sound.

—LONGFELLOW

I SOUGHT OUT A SMALL HOTEL the proprietor of which was a Portuguese. Much to my surprise, it had a bath—a vast cement sarcophagus—for, mindful of my experience at Kisenyi, I fully expected to be told that there was a nice big river just outside, as indeed there was, the Congo itself, which is about a mile wide here.

The Congo, 3000 miles long, is the seventh longest river in the world, and the fact that it was a mile wide at this point, 1000 miles from its mouth, was very impressive. It is navigated by steamers of 500 tons between here and Leopoldville, distant 200 miles from the coast. The journey takes eleven days coming upstream, and nine going down. A mile above Stanleyville navigation is prevented by the Stanley Falls, but the gap of eighty miles is bridged by a railway, while beyond, vessels of 150 tons ply as far as Kindu, 200 miles away. From there by means of rail and river (still the Congo, although called the Lualaba) it is now possible to reach the east coast via Lake Tanganyika and the Central Railway; the west coast by the Benguela Railway; and Cape Town by railway via Elisabethville. That town is the centre of the rich mining district of Katanga, on the Belgian Congo-Northern Rhodesia border. Copper is the chief product, but uranium ore, the source of radium, is also mined there.

Stanleyville had a half-begun, half-finished sort of air. The trade depression was then being felt severely; everything seemed to be in a state of suspended animation. There were great wide avenues beautifully planted with ornamental trees, which bore grandiloquent names such as 'The Avenue of the Grand Duke,' but which contained either nothing at all, or perhaps a solitary grass hut.

I spent the day looking round the town, removing some of the sand and grit from the bearings of the bicycle, changing a tyre, and procuring some information from the British Consul about my next immediate objective. I could, of course, have reached the coast by river steamer, but as the fare was over 1000 francs—of which amount I was 800 francs short—it was satisfactory to learn that there was an alternative route, albeit a long one. This alternative road led north to Bangassu, in French Equatorial Africa, before it turned westwards through the French Cameroons, to finally reach the coast at a little port called Kribi. This information was not all available at Stanleyville; all I could learn there was that there was a road as far as Bangassu, so to Bangassu I determined to go.

Like the Kivu-Stanleyville road by which I had come, this road to Bangassu and beyond was of recent construction. Since the War, communications in all parts of Africa have been extended with extraordinary rapidity. Kipling, in one of his stories, affirms that 'transportation is civilisation,' and if it is as simple as that, then the nations of Europe, however mixed their motives, are rapidly civilising Africa.

I intended having two days' rest at Stanleyville, because a painful boil seemed to hint that something of the sort was advisable. There was, however, little of interest in the town, and the boil was not on a part vital to a cyclist, so I pushed on again after only one. My Portuguese host very kindly got up himself to give me an early breakfast, and speed me on my way with a present of oranges. This was not the only instance of Portuguese kindness which I shall have to record.

At the next halt I watched with interest a local chair-making industry. The wood used was, I think, mahogany, the design original and beautifully simple. There were no legs, only two pieces of wood. The piece for the back, about four feet long and eighteen inches wide, was slightly hollowed, with a horizontal slit a foot from its lower end through which the second piece was passed. One end of the latter rested on the ground behind the back as a support, the other end, also slightly hollowed, forming the seat. The finished article was comfortable and very good to look at.

Assisted by a moon just past the full, I was making very early starts, and the following day I took the road soon after 4 a.m. Once the sun rose above the horizon little grace was allowed. Minute by minute the heat increased, becoming within a short two hours so gruelling that the flesh grew weary and the spirit drooped at the bare thought of the yet distant noontide.

About eleven o'clock a loud report indicated a flat tyre. It was more of a burst than a puncture, and proved to be the first of a rapid series, until I discovered the cause. The tyres bore the words 'inflate hard,' an injunction I was following too faithfully, allowing nothing for the expansion of the air inside caused by the increasing heat. The spare tubes came in handy now, for, as it was quite impossible to make a patch stick in the daytime, another tube had to be fitted, and any repairs made at night.

My old acquaintance the Ituri River, cropping up again after a change of course, welcomed me with a pest which was new to me and which made it difficult to suffer with patience a long wait for the ferry. It was a very small bluish fly which settled on the bare skin and drew blood. As I was wearing no socks or stockings, and my shirt-sleeves were rolled up, I was an easy prey, and soon legs and arms were streaked with blood. I met it again later on, but it seemed to occur only in the vicinity of rivers.

I was now north of the equator, having already twice crossed it, and, although the sun was well to the south, the temperature seemed to be increasing, due no doubt to a gradual fall in the country, which was now only about 1500 feet above sea level.

The next place I reached of any note was Buta, 200 miles north of Stanleyville. It boasts two banks and some half-dozen trading-houses, and it is connected by road with Rejaf, in the Sudan. It is this highway which is used by cars travelling from Uganda to Nigeria or the Sahara. In spite of the comparative importance of Buta, I was unable to change my Belgian Congo francs for French Congo francs, or to obtain any quinine or tobacco. Situated as I was, I regarded these two as essentials—particularly the quinine, which was at length provided by a Government hospital, but only after I had filled in more forms than would have been necessary had I been getting buried. For my pipe I was reduced to using disintegrated *caporal* cigarettes. I was told (and it was the truth) that no banks existed between here and the coast, but I managed to pick up some French money from a Greek storekeeper.

He came from Cyprus, and when he discovered that I was English, and therefore a fellow-subject, he not only changed my money but gave me a lot of oranges.

Soon after leaving Buta, I made an unnecessarily long halt at midday in a little wayside store kept by a 'coast boy,' a native of Nigeria and therefore another fellow-subject. He delighted in airing his pidgin-English, and, being of more than average intelligence, also spoke French, Swahili, and Bangalla, the language used in the northern part of the Congo. Swahili, the lingua franca of East Africa, was at length beginning to fail me as a conversational medium. Up to Stanleyville it had served me well.

A sufficiently belated start was further delayed by the discovery of a flat back tyre just as I was going to mount. It was a burst almost too big to patch, and I cursed my stupidity for not having changed the tube when I changed the tyre at Buta. 'A new cover deserves a new tube' is as sound a rule for cyclists as for motorists. Remembering the struggle I had had in removing the back wheel, I did not welcome a repetition, so I put patch over patch, with an all-embracing one over everything for luck, and rode off in fear and trembling. I need not have worried. That remarkable bit of work lasted the remaining 250 miles to Bangassu, where I was able to buy another tube.

Still going north and slightly west, I rejoiced to see the forest giving way gradually to more open country. I felt like a swimmer coming to the surface after prolonged submersion. The road was becoming more hilly, too, offering me at odd times distant views which did something to compensate me for the extra pushing thus entailed. Otherwise my field of vision was restricted, as before, to the road. The country was covered in elephant grass ten feet high, which was just as difficult to see over as the 150 feet high walls of the forest.

As forest gave way to grassland, the cultivated areas became more extensive. The palm-oil tree, whose products, together with cotton and sesame, are exported, was seen for the first time. Sesame, a small oil-producing seed, used sometimes as a relish with bananas, is a highly concentrated food-stuff.

Hunting, however, seemed a more popular industry than agriculture, for nearly every native carried some sort of weapon—the less wealthy or more conservative a sort of cross-bow, the others an antiquated firearm. Game was apparently plentiful, and there were no restrictions, but, although the long grass makes hunting difficult, thereby prolonging the animal life and the industry, yet when the grass is burnt off in the dry weather the harassed game must fall an easy prey to the multitude of hunters. No game will survive long in these conditions.

At the village at which I stopped, the headman insisted on providing me with a guard of two arque-busiers. I assumed, mistakenly as it turned out, that this was because I was back in a game country, but he later explained that it was not so much the dangerous game he feared as the thieving propensities of his fellow-villagers. I like to think that he misjudged them, for I lost nothing here nor anywhere else. Once, when I dropped a spanner, a boy chased me for a mile to return it.

The crossing of another large river brought me to Bonda, another trading centre, surrounded by extensive cultivation-oil palms, cotton, and sesame. On leaving Bonda, taking advantage of a good road and a heavily overcast sky, I put in a very long day during which I covered eighty miles. This distance was only done by carrying on until a too late hour—a folly for which I paid with a poor billet where there were very few bananas and no eggs. As these were my mainstays, both dinner and breakfast would not have embarrassed an ascetic, while, to make matters worse, at the latter cheerless meal, taken in candle-light, I made the pleasing discovery that a tyre was flat and the pump missing. No doubt it had been shaken off at one of those many places where it had been a matter for surprise that anything, including the rider, had been left on.

My mood was one of the deepest gloom as I trundled the bike slowly along. I was very empty, and I was uncertain whether I should have to push it for 1000 miles or only 100 miles before finding another pump. Five miles on, I saw an obvious mission perched on a high hill half a mile from the road, where a passing boy told me that the missionary had a bicycle. I went up there, to have matters soon put right and to be given a meal by the Norwegian missionary and his wife. It was one of the Basle Missions. Apart from the relief of being once more mobile, I found it refreshing to be on a hill again and to look out upon surrounding country after so many days' confinement in a tunnel of vegetation.

A little further on was Monga, which, although the French Boundary is another fifty miles north, is the last post in Belgian territory. I
discovered that there was a customs barrier here, in charge of a Belgian
official to whom I should have to present myself for examination. I
was rather conscience-stricken and not a little worried, because I had
been travelling in the Congo for three weeks and was now about to
leave it without having made my presence known to anyone officially.
The official concerned was rather shocked when I made this confes-
sion, but, to my surprise, accepted the fact cheerfully and passed me
through without any fuss. I left the Belgian Congo with a very favourable impression of at least one official. I was soon to learn that, in the
French colonies, the way of the stranger was hard, being the subject
of a tiresome official scrutiny which in the Belgian had been conspicuously absent.

The frontier between the Belgian Congo and French territory is
the Ubangi River. The French colony, called by them Afrique Equatori-
ale Française, or A.E.F. for short, comprises a very large area stretching
over twenty-seven degrees of latitude. In such a vast area conditions
must necessarily vary greatly, but in the Ubangi-Shari province which
I traversed they are similar to those in the northern Congo. The total
white population in 1926 was 2500, and the natives numbered over
3,000,000, two-thirds of which occupied the relatively remote northern provinces of Chad and Ubangi-Shari.

I reached the Ubangi River and the frontier on a sweltering
hot afternoon, hot enough to provide reasonable mortals with every
excuse for sleep. French officialdom, however, was very wide awake.
The canoe in which I crossed had barely grounded before I was surrounded by a cloud of black myrmidons demanding that I should
present myself forthwith before the respective heads of the administration, the customs, and the police. On a hot afternoon, after a
sixty-mile ride, I found it an overpowering welcome. As I was aware
that my streaming face and shabby shirt would not make a good
impression, I asked for time to put on the clean shirt kept for such
emergencies. But no respite was allowed. I had to present myself as
I was, all dust and sweat, to explain in halting French whence I had
come, whither I was going, and even more vital questions, such as my
mother's maiden name and the Christian names of both my parents.

(I am told that this is done to find if one has any remote German connections.)

M. le Commandant at the bureau was polite and helpful, but all this information had to be laboriously entered on various forms before I was given a *laissez-passer*. At the customs they were less polite and not at all helpful. The 'big shot' was not at the office, and when I suggested going away to look for food and lodging before returning later, his black henchmen would not hear of it, but promptly impounded the bicycle, the rucksack, and myself. When the chief did come at five o'clock, he was rather peeved at being expected to transact business at that hour. We were not at all *en rapport*, and in the end the vileness of my French and the lateness of the hour so exasperated him that he detained me there over the weekend while he filled in the necessary forms for one bicycle in transit—what he called a *vélocipède*.

There was a European-owned store here where I was lucky enough to find a pump and to be able to change both tyres. But that was not done till next day, as at the moment I wanted food and drink. Having procured with some difficulty a bottle of beer and a few eggs, I repaired to the rest-house in the dark, where a boy volunteered to bring wood and water. As there was no chair and no bed, a brick floor was again my portion. Pending the arrival of the wood and water, I tackled the beer-bottle. The top refused to budge, so, losing what little temper the customs officer had left me, I tried to knock the neck off, with the result that the whole thing exploded, leaving behind nothing but a cut finger, a mess upon the floor, and a fragrant memory. I forget how many francs it had cost—enough, anyway, to preclude the possibility of buying another.

There was nothing remarkable in the tiny station of Bangassu except the rudeness of the customs man, the inhospitality of the half-dozen inhabitants, and a diminutive racecourse with the most hair-raising bends I have ever seen. There is a racecourse at Darjeeling which is circular—all bend and no straight—but this one seemed to be all straight, with the bends right angles. I saw no horses, but further north, where the country is drier and more open, they are common. Since leaving Ankole, the only livestock I had seen had been goats and pigs, but I had been told some cows were kept on a farm near Stanley-ville to supply the town with milk. Most of the goats seemed to be of a very good type. Three kids to one nanny goat was a common sight, and at one or two places I was given goats' milk, a luxury never had in Kenya, where goats swarm.

After two nights on the brick floor of the rest-house I was ready, anxious almost, to start for my next objective. This was Bangui, a town lower down the Ubangi River, but only to be reached by traversing 500 miles of road of unknown quality. I had been warned not to expect such good roads after leaving the Belgian Congo, where the road had fully justified the good accounts I had heard of it. Motor traffic, for which the road was made, cannot expect much better, and the fact that on a cycle one could average between fifty miles and sixty miles a day for 1000 miles through a small corner of the Congo is striking testimony to the energy and skill which went to its making. To carry a road over escarpments, across many big rivers, and multitudinous small streams, through swamps and dense forests, aided only by a scanty and half savage population, is a task worthy of a General Wade or a Macadam. In the Congo the trunk roads are confined to the north-east corner; in the centre and west the rivers, helped out by short stretches of rail, are the only means of communication between distant places. In a relatively short time much development has been accomplished, but as yet only the fringe has been touched. Further expansion depends on more roads and more railways, the provision of which must be necessarily a slow and costly business, owing to the difficulties of the terrain and the sparse population. In an area of 918,000 square miles there are only 9,000,000 natives, whereas in Nigeria, which is less than half the area, there are 20,000,000. However, the Congo is better off in this respect than French Equatorial Africa, where for the same area there are only 3,000,000 natives.

In passing from Belgian to French territory, little change was to be noted, nor was it to be expected by the mere crossing from the south side of the Ubangi River to the north. The natives and the scenery appeared the same, and I longed in vain for some break in the ever recurring ridge and valley covered with the same long elephant grass, which was by now almost as monotonous as the forest. The road was slightly worse, but at first by no means bad, although later it deteriorated. The French seemingly had less regard for grading than the Belgian engineers, charging their hills in a very uncompromising manner.

This neglect of grading gave rise to much 'wash,' producing a surface scored and rutted with deep channels. In Uganda, and possibly in the Congo, too, the system used for the making of a road is to dig two trenches, each about two feet wide, the width of a wheel-track apart. These are then filled with big stones, and the whole surface of the road, not much wider than the wheel-tracks, is then covered with murram. This murram is a sort of red gravel which seems to form the subsoil, almost without a break, from Uganda to the west coast. When well beaten down it makes a fair surface. (The best going for a bicycle was generally, not on the road, but on a footpath made and worn smooth by native use, which carefully avoids the road on account of the unkindliness of murram for bare feet.) This system ensured that the portion of road which carried the weight of traffic was well ballasted, and was at the same time economical.

The Belgians employed permanent labour, established in the *cantonniers*, for road maintenance, but the French seemed to rely only upon the villagers. Judging by the state of the road, and by the few gangs I saw at work, this system was inefficient and unpopular. With each gang there was an askari, or native soldier, armed with rifle and bayonet to back the authority of the headman who carried a mighty whip. A minor point that interested me was that between Bangassu and Bangui there were no kilometre posts. I knew not whether to repine or rejoice. Long before Stanleyville was reached, it had become a debatable point whether the advantage of knowing the length of the day's run outweighed the accumulatively depressing effect of counting them.

Little change was discernible either in the natives, their huts, or their mode of life, but there was one variation which affected me personally—namely, that Swahili was no longer understood. The officials at Bangassu had assured me that most of the village headmen could talk French—a fact that I am prepared to believe, but it was not the sort that I could understand. As my own is of 'the pen of my aunt's gardener' variety, the fault, perhaps, was not entirely theirs. As my wants were few and simple I managed well enough, but much of the interest of travel is lost if one cannot talk to the inhabitants.

Another not unimportant change for me was that bananas seemed now to be grown only as a luxury, for the staple food was manioc, or cassava. This is a tuber which has to be prepared for eating by fermentation and drying. The first process seemed to be never-ending, as every village stank like a bag of maize meal which has got wet and gone bad.

My second day in A.E.F. saw a marked deterioration in the road and a great reduction in the number of villages, the last fact probably accounting for the bad road. Not even the most perfunctory attempt at grading had been made, as the guiding principle appeared to be that valleys, of which there were many, existed only to be crossed. The end of a gruelling day found me in a disgustingly dirty village. A boy who spoke Swahili, having served in East Africa during the War, advised me to go to a mission a little further on, and this I did. I had avoided missions so far except on two occasions, partly on account of the difficulty of making an early start without disturbing my hosts, and partly because, having contributed nothing to missions in the past, it seemed unfair for me to make use of them now. It was another of the Basle Missions kept by a Norwegian and his Swiss wife, who received me very kindly. They had a small, frail-looking child, and they told me that they had buried four other children there, a fact which was eloquent enough testimony to a villainous climate. From the Congo to the Cameroons there is little to choose from in the way of climate; most of the country is under 2000 feet, very hot, and the rainfall heavy.

During the course of the evening, I heard a good deal about the country from the missionary, who spoke English well. I was told that the construction of the road had advanced to this point only in 1925, and that the natives were still rather wild and intractable. Among other unpleasant traits was some skill in the use of poisons, while they had a burial custom which struck me as being more revolting than cannibalism. They boiled the corpse gently until only the bones were left, the resulting soup being then drunk by the sorrowing friends and relatives. These kind people (I mean the missionaries, not the soup-drinkers) gave me a lot of dried bananas, an excellent sustaining food, to take with me. These are prepared by baking ripe bananas until they are quite brown and tough, in which state they will keep indefinitely. At this mission work was regarded as second only to prayer. There were one hundred acres of coffee demanding attention from the mission's adherents, with the result that the day began early, thus allowing of my leaving before seven without making myself a nuisance to my hosts.

The following night I enjoyed yet more hospitality at the camp of three French gold prospectors. From the comfort of their quarters, their dinner, and the two bottles of St. Julien which accompanied it, I concluded that they were employed by a wealthy company and were not free-lances. It rained and thundered furiously in the night, and was still so doing when I left before dawn. The road was mostly under water, but I found good going on a native footpath on the far side of the deep drainage ditch which lined the road. It cleared about midday, when I reached Bambari, a small trading centre where there was a store and a cotton ginnery. Here the flood of hospitality, which had set in at the mission, reached its height, almost overwhelming me.

I stopped at the store, the only one of its kind between Bangassu and Bangui, hoping to get some bread. The owner was a Portuguese. He had no bread to sell, but gave me a small roll gratis. Touched by this kindness, I thought to repay it by buying a bottle of his red wine, but, not to be outdone, the man from Portugal then invited me to lunch. On the veranda of his hut there were two fellow-guests, a Russian and an Italian, who had come to buy cotton, although at the moment they were drinking whisky. It was a hot day (they were all that, but this one was what John Jorrocks would have called 'uncommon 'ot') but, in spite of that and the time of day, I was invited to help myself. They braced themselves to see me knock back a neat tumblerful, for foreigners seem to expect an Englishman to mop up whisky like water at any hour of the day or night. Possibly this is because they fail to differentiate between Englishmen and Scotsmen, the latter, of course, being far the more numerous of the two in these outlandish places. Another curious thing is that out in Africa most foreigners—Frenchmen, Belgians, Greeks, Portuguese—drink whisky, whereas at home probably none of them would think of touching it. It is perhaps less expensive for them in Africa than in their own countries, but, besides that, they regard it as the most suitable drink for a hot climate; I remember a Frenchman becoming quite lyrical over its properties, both medicinal and convivial.

Well, there were my friends, waiting goggle-eyed with apprehension for the Englishman to swallow unblinkingly, in the national manner, a terrific dose of whisky, and great was their astonishment, amounting almost to horror, when he refused to take any. This refusal cost me a good deal of prestige which a glass of port, accepted as the lesser of two evils, did little to restore. With the arrival of a Belgian, a Frenchman, and the Portuguese storekeeper's brother, the party was complete, so that when we gathered round the table, Russian, Frenchman, Belgian, Italian, two Portuguese, and an Englishman, but for the more convivial atmosphere prevailing we might have been mistaken for a meeting of the League of Nations Assembly.

The meal was tremendous. It began with a sort of olla podrida, passed on to the flesh of some unknown animal, followed that with duck, salad, and a sweet, and ended with some pungent Roquefort cheese. We drank a rough red wine and 'topped up' with coffee laced with more whisky. It would have been impolite to ask, but I was curious to know whether this was my host's usual midday meal, or whether it was a banquet specially prepared to facilitate a deal in cotton which he apparently concluded satisfactorily by an exchange of signatures with the Italian; whatever it was, I for one could say, 'Fate cannot harm me—I have dined today.'

By four o'clock, I had recovered the use of some of my faculties and rode gently on for fifteen miles, musing on life's vicissitudes. The village where I finally fell off was the home of the local chief, who lived in dignified seclusion behind a tall reed fence. He did not show himself to the stranger within his gates, sending me instead a present of six bad eggs, but with this exception the natives here seemed quite uncivilised. They brought wood and water before I asked for it, and put an empty hut at my disposal, which, now that I was beyond the tick-infested area, I was not afraid of using. In addition to the snack which I had had for lunch, that was a red-letter day for other reasons. Since leaving Bangassu I had seen only two lorries, both of them in Bambari, the scene of the orgy. Here, in the village, I noticed a bicycle, and, still a little muddled, half expected to see a sign, 'Teas and Accommodation for Cyclists.'

Next day I passed through a small administrative post called Gumari, where, anxious though I was to avoid officialdom, I was trapped by an officious native clerk into paying a visit to the commandant. This clerk who accosted me was so curious and suspicious that he considered it his duty to introduce me to M. le Commandant, who was busy hearing cases in the court. To create a diversion I sent him to the market to find some oranges, playing thus all unknowingly into his hands, for presently he returned with a great basket full of oranges which he declared were a present from the commandant. I could hardly ignore this, untrue though I felt it to be, and was led meekly to the Presence. The course of justice was suspended while the commandant took me away to be introduced to his wife and family; my plea for mercy, or at least a respite, on the grounds of dirtiness, was of no avail, because he himself sported a three-day beard. Neither he nor his wife had any English, but we drank beer and battled away for an hour or more before I could decently escape. Outside, the black promoter of sociability amongst the whites was still waiting for me, carrying the *fons et origo malorum*, of which I could only take away a dozen—the sole fruits of two hours' delay.

The lost time was made up by the cutting short of my midday halt. This happened to be at a rest-house, a building which usually ensured for one a little privacy, but here the crowd showed no respect even for that. They invaded it and refused to be driven out, so that I was forced to flee. The crowd nuisance was aggravated or mitigated according to the degree of control exercised by the headman—or *capita*, as he was called—of the village. He was responsible for the rest-house and for the providing of anyone who occupied it with wood and water, so that the occupant had some official standing. Some of these headmen had their people well in hand, but others were completely ineffective. There was an amusing example of the former type that same night when the headman of the village at which I stopped, seeing a woman going past with a load of wood, commandeered it for my use. Pleased with this show of authority, he turned to continue his chat with me, but no sooner was his back turned than the old woman recommandeered her load. Unfortunately, before going far she was spotted by the irate headman, who gave chase and dealt out summary punishment. The custom was to pay the *capita* a fixed rate for supplying wood and water—a very satisfactory arrangement no doubt for him, but highly unsatisfactory for the hewers and drawers of these necessities.

As I drew near to Bangui I was again seized with the same feverish impatience which beset me approaching Stanleyville. A sequence of long days was brought to an end with twelve hours of almost continuous riding in which nearly eighty miles were covered. I arrived in a deluge of warm rain.

CHAPTER XVII

WESTWARDS TO THE ATLANTIC

Men to holloa and men to run him.

—MASEFIELD

BANGUI BOASTED A SMALL HOTEL whose proprietor was not too proud to receive me as a guest in spite of my ruffianly appearance—an appearance perhaps best described as travel-stained. The beer (which was iced) exceeded my wildest expectations, but the bath was an anti-climax. For this, a boy conducted me to an outhouse with a bare floor but no sign of a bath. On my telling the boy to hurry up and bring it, he pointed with smiling satisfaction to the ceiling, whence hung a small perforated bucket. Pulling a string, he released on me a feeble, short-lived shower, of the same temperature as, but of considerably less violence than, the storm in which I had arrived.

It was a Sunday evening, and it seemed to me that the whole of the European population of Bangui, numbering about three hundred, were assembled on the terrace outside, drinking *apéritifs* and talking as only Frenchmen can talk. I had forgotten there were so many white people in Africa, and that some of them could be as noisy and as voluble as the natives.

Bangui is the second town in importance in French Equatorial Africa. The capital town is Brazzaville, on the opposite bank of the Congo to Leopoldville, which is the capital of the Belgian Congo. From Bangui down to Brazzaville is ten days' steaming by river steamer. In addition to this outlet by river there is a road to Yaunde, in the French Cameroons, 740 miles away. A transport company has a contract with the Government to maintain a fortnightly lorry service on this road for the conveyance of mails and passengers, the journey taking five days and costing three thousand francs. Owing to Bangui's remote situation, its trade is comparatively small, so that the population consists mostly of officials. A big military aerodrome and a wireless station lend it some importance. The climate is warm and not particularly healthy, as the town is situated on the river-bank itself; rather unnecessarily in my opinion, because, less than a mile away, are some hills 200 or 300 feet high, where the residential quarter could have been built with advantage.

I spent two days resting here. On the afternoon after my arrival, while I was 'taking mine ease in mine inn,' Falstaff-like, my tranquility was rudely shattered by a very brusque French policeman who wanted to know why I had not yet reported my arrival. His manner was so peremptory that I was a bit short with him, and both of us began to get heated. My passport and the *laissez-passer* which had been given me at Bangassu failed to pacify him, and he intimated that the debate, now very warm, would be continued at the local lock-up. Luckily, my host, who was standing by, seeing how things were going, suggested a drink. Quickly taking the hint, I ordered unlimited iced beer, which soon had a cooling effect upon the wrath of the policeman, who presently began pledging the Entente Cordiale, whose existence he deplored having momentarily forgotten.

I made an early start when I left Bangui. I breakfasted off some hard-boiled eggs and red wine which I had had placed in my room, with the result that I soon began to feel queer—it takes a Frenchman to drink red wine at dawn. I felt weak and muzzy all morning, but fortunately the road was flat and ran perfectly straight through forty-five miles of oil palm forest. I lunched at the hut of a War veteran who had fought in the Cameroons campaign. He repaid the interest I showed by mending my shirt, both sleeves of which had come adrift where they had been chafed by the rucksack straps.

Stopping that night at a little post called Mbaiki, I had occasion to reconsider the low opinion of French officials which I had formed. I was treated in a way that more than atoned for the little unpleasantness at Bangui, but my benefactor, although in charge of the district, was an army officer, not a civilian. In the less settled parts of French Equatorial Africa the administration is in the hands of the army, and Mbaiki was the headquarters of a district in charge of a captain who was the local Pooh-Bah—Judge, Policeman, Commandant, and Lord High Muck-a-Muck. He had with him half his company of native soldiers (askaris), while the other half under two white subalterns was stationed in other parts of the district.

As soon as he heard of my arrival he sent along a camp-bed and an invitation to dinner. He had served in France during the War and in most parts of French Africa since, so that in listening to him the evening passed very pleasantly. He spoke no English, and as my French might be described as passive rather than active, he had to do most of the talking. According to him, their best recruiting-ground was the Province of Lake Chad, west of the Sudan, the natives of the country round Bangui or nearer the coast being of little value as soldiers. The native soldier, he told me, greatly looks forward to doing a tour of duty in France (I presume he meant in peace-time), and if a man's record is good he can serve for fifteen years, after which he is entitled to a pension of eighty francs—the equivalent of about two shillings a month, an amount seemingly insufficient to keep a man in tobacco, but on which a native can live quite comfortably.

Although the dinner was not in the grand Portuguese manner, it was ample. In place of coffee we drank citronella tea, an infusion made from a grass which is here planted extensively by the roadside as a border to check 'wash.' The tea is a pleasant, mildly lemon-flavoured drink supposed to have medicinal properties. It is a curious fact that while there are several varieties of 'tea' which in addition to being quite pleasant to drink are also reputed to be 'good for one,' that which is drunk almost universally is the one that has no pretensions to being anything but mildly poisonous. Either we are difficult to please or have a deal of innate perversity.

The broken, hilly country of long grass with scattered forest continued unaltered, failing by its monotony, like the Congo forest, to arouse any feeling but dislike. If the scenery was the same, the road surface was full of variety, claiming, with the many hills, a single-minded devotion from the traveller. That day there was one particularly vile stretch of sand-surfaced road on which I executed many 'voluntaries.'

It was about this time, too, that my popularity as a public spectacle was at its height. On the second night from Bangui the natives invaded my quarters and would not be ejected. They fought for front seats, while I took my food like a lion at the Zoo but without the protecting bars. That was bad, but next day this staring business reached a climax, so that for the next forty-eight hours I thought I had reached a country of Bedlamites. It sounds merely funny now, but at the time it nearly drove me frantic: possibly my sense of humour was becoming a little blunted now that I had acted the part of a travelling circus for so long.

The trouble started at a midday halt, where a crowd gathered to see the bicycle and to watch me eat. It need hardly be said that that was nothing unusual; indeed, by now I was quite accustomed to eating and drinking, getting up and going to bed, watched by an astonished crowd like the Grand Monarch at a levee. This time, however, when I re-started, the crowd started, too, so that I pedalled down the road surrounded by the whole village, laughing and yelling like madmen. Thinking they would soon tire, I rode fast to shake them off, only to be easily caught up with on the hills. Nothing would induce them to stop. Scowls, threats, curses, and attempts to ride them down only made them more excited. Long before the human pack began to tire and tail off, hunted and hunters had reached another village, whose people, incited by the approaching cry, were not slow to catch the infection, and turned out fresh and fit to take up the running. Changing foxes in the middle of a run is the huntsman's *bête noir*; but what would the fox think—what could I think—of changing packs?

I had to stop somewhere; I could not go on riding all night; but at the first village where I pulled up the mob exceeded all others in size, curiosity, and determination. Bear gardens, bargain counters, jumble sales, are all weak similes with which to liken the scene in that rest-house (what irony to call it that!). Goaded at last to desperation, I ran amok with a stick, and, having cleared a passage, rode off in the gathering darkness to camp foodless, but in peace, by the roadside.

On the following morning this harassing pursuit flared up again for a time, until it stopped, almost as suddenly as it began, at a village where I was received with a quiet which was, by reason of its contrast, well-nigh stunning. A few grave elders were the only ones to approach, the common herd attending strictly to its business, and when I thought the notables had gazed their fill, a mild 'Allez-vous' was sufficient to disperse them.

The reasons for this extraordinary outbreak are obscure. The only theory I have is that these particular villages had only recently been built and occupied by natives brought in from some outlying district. As has already been noted, the administrative policy in the Congo and in parts of A.E.F. is to collect the natives in villages along the roadside, in the first place to make the road, thereafter for its maintenance, and to facilitate the work of the district officers. For unless the natives are within reach of a road they are to all intents and purposes non-existent from an administrative point of view, so difficult is movement away from the road. It is understandable that to a raw native the astounding spectacle of a white man carrying a load, riding along miraculously balanced on two wheels, was not likely to be repeated in his lifetime, so that it was worth more than a passing glance. Imagine the case of a black man in native dress stalking into a village in England to stand, say, on one leg, leaning on a spear, in the attitude beloved of Nilotic negroes. How the children would guy the poor fellow, chivying him to the next village, while even their elders might leave their beer for an unguarded moment to know the meaning of it.

That these particular natives were scarcely human—people who, according to Darwin, had not long come down from their trees—could be inferred not only from their odd sense of humour, but also from their huts, which were of that primitive beehive type last seen by me on top of the Kabasha escarpment. The villages appeared to have been constructed only recently. They were big, dirty, rather miserable-looking places, all as like as peas, with the huts arranged in two well-spaced parallel lines. They had obviously been laid out to order, while the fact that as yet there were no banana-trees or pawpaws was an indication of their recent origin. Lean, long-snouted, black pigs ran about scavenging like pariah dogs.

Rather more than half-way to Yaunde is Berbarati, an administrative post, where I stopped for the night. It was a fairly big place, with a rest-house and a store at which, however, I could buy nothing. Returning disconsolate to the rest-house, I was met by a boy bearing a basket of oranges with the 'compliments of M. le Commandant.' This was a familiar gambit, but in the circumstances an invitation to a meal, or the offer of even a loaf of bread, would have been more than welcome. Half expecting something of the kind, I put on my spare shirt and walked round to pay my respects, but the only invitation I received was one to produce my passport forthwith.

The following day I reached Gombola, on the border between A.E.F. and the French Cameroons, where curiously enough there is a customs barrier. We are not quite so stupid in the management of our East African Colonies. True, the three adjacent territories of Kenya, Uganda, and Tanganyika has each its separate, expensive, and jealous government, but there is at any rate a customs and postal union.

I had been warned of the *douanier* in charge at Gombola when I was at distant Bangui, where they said he was mad. Sane customs officials can be awkward enough, but imagination boggles at the thought of being examined by a mad one. I therefore assumed what I thought was an ingratiating manner, but on approaching the enemy with the utmost trepidation, we almost fell on each other's necks. There is a proverb to the effect that 'like draws to like the whole world over,' which is perhaps some explanation of the favour I found, but I prefer to think that he only feigned madness the better to carry out his disagreeable duties, and that, like Hamlet, he 'knew a hawk from a handsaw.' Indeed, when I told him where I had come from and what I was doing, I thought he was going to kiss me, but he thought better of it, and, instead, passed me and my bicycle through at a cost of forty centimes in as many seconds, giving me a bunch of bananas three feet long into the bargain. While talking he told me that on an average he examined only two vehicles a day, but he managed to fill his leisure hours with gardening and bird-shooting. He also assured me that the road through the Cameroons was so perfect that I should just *rouler* (French, I suppose, for free-wheel) to the coast. At that I mounted hastily, thinking that perhaps my informants at Bangui were right after all.

On crossing this artificial frontier, I found no marked change of scenery. Further west the country became more hilly and the elevation gradually increased, until at Yaunde a height of 2500 feet above sea level was reached. There was one minor but rather curious difference, which was that, once I had entered the Cameroons, I no longer found chairs in the villages. For the midday halt I therefore reverted to the roadside, gaining in privacy and losing nothing in comfort. My first halt in this way was shared by a Polish lorry-driver who spoke excellent American. He was bound for Yaunde, still 300 miles away, and offered me a lift, which I was obliged to refuse, for it had now become a point of honour with me to finish the journey unaided. From the first he had,

I think, entertained doubts as to my sanity—doubts which this refusal fully confirmed.

Batouri, which I reached a day later, was the first administrative post in the Cameroons, and, knowing by now the vigilance of the French authorities, I took the trouble to report my arrival to M. le Commandant. The Polish lorry-driver who preceded me there must have talked, because I was received with the soothing manner reserved only for the very rich or the very eccentric. Even my proffered passport was waved aside.

The Cameroons were, of course, a German colony before the War, and are now under French and British mandates. The French portion is very much larger than the British, comprising 166,489 square miles against 34,236 square miles, the respective populations being two million and seven hundred thousand. The name 'Cameroons' is derived from a river which was called by the early Portuguese navigators the Cameroes River, meaning the river of prawns.

In the Cameroons I first began to hear 'pidgin' or 'coast' English spoken. The usual greeting was now 'Morning' instead of what had always sounded to me like 'Bon soir.' As this expression was used regardless of the time of day, I found it a bit disconcerting to be greeted with 'Bon soir' at dawn. 'Pidgin' English, which has for long been the *lingua franca* of the west coast, has now spread far inland; it was used by the Germans, and is used now by the French traders, who could not get on very well without it. I believe the Germans, with their usual thoroughness, had published a German-'Pidgin' dictionary. I myself felt the need of something of the kind, for this curious jargon is not so easy to understand as might be imagined, even for an Englishman. There are familiar words which mean something else, such as 'chop' meaning food, and 'dash' a present. The last word is also used as a verb, for when one gives a boy a tip one speaks of 'dashing' him. 'Lib,' which I suppose is the west coast way of pronouncing 'live,' is a very hard-used word—'him no lib' means 'it is not here' and 'him lib for die' means 'he is going to die.'

The approaching completion of any important stage on the journey always filled me with nervous impatience, and now I was becoming all worked up at the proximity of Yaunde, which marked, if not quite the end of the journey, at least the end of all difficulties. I had been on the road now for forty-five days, and I congratulated myself that I was crossing Africa at its waist, so to speak, south of the great bulge, thereby saving myself an extra thousand miles.

My starts became earlier and earlier. On November 1st I was on the road so early that, being unable to see the road properly, I took three spills in quick succession. Dawn brought with it a storm which burst on me and which, with the perversity of storms, travelled in the same direction as the road, so that I rode all day through rain and mist over a wet, heavy surface. At the unusually early hour of 3.30 p.m., when I reached a small administrative post, I decided to call it a day. I found shelter in a good rest-house where there was a table, several string beds, and a caretaker who spoke 'pidgin,' so that after a meal eaten off a table I turned in early, anticipating a good night on a bed. It was good until midnight, when a lorry drew up to disgorge three missionaries. Their leader woke me by flashing a torch in my face and began a shorter catechism as to who I was and what I was doing. He then reviewed briefly his own antecedents, told me his late arrival was due to a broken bridge, and proceeded to unfold his plans for the immediate future. I tried to discourage his proposal to pass the rest of the night at the rest-house by pointing out the lateness of the hour and the probabilities of my disturbing them when I started at 4 a.m. But that was simply playing into the hands of this masterful man, for I was quickly informed that he himself was getting up at 3.30 a.m., and would I mind leaving the table clear for him to celebrate Mass before they left. At that hour I was awake myself. As the Church still snored, I got up to start breakfast even at the risk of upsetting the time-table. When the zealot did wake, the sight of my eating eggs provoked him to fury. He routed out his two companions with scant ceremony, shouted to his boys to load the lorry, and presently the whole party had disappeared, furious and fasting, in a metaphorical cloud of smoke.

On the following day, helped by a moon near the full, I started even earlier to do fifty miles before halting at midday. Determined to make a day of it, I pushed on again at one o'clock, disregarding the fierce sun, and at five o'clock entered upon a long stretch of flat, swampy country where there were no villages but plenty of mosquitoes. It was dark before I found a village where I hoped to get some food. My plan was to take advantage of the moon and ride all night, but, fortunately, while I was still eating it began raining hard, thus obliterating the moon and with it my fatuous proposal. I found quarters for the night in the hut of a very helpful mission boy who, with his family, vacated half their hut to leave it at my disposal, but I was too restless to sleep much. At 1 a.m. I breakfasted, shaved, and put on my best shirt in anticipation of Yaunde, bestowing the old one on my host. By 2 a.m. I was on the road again—a road made soft and sticky by the rain.

There was a grain of method in this seeming madness because, the day being Saturday, I was anxious to reach Yaunde by midday before the post office closed down for the weekend. A moment's reflection would, however, have reassured me, for in French Colonies the week-end habit is not observed with the scrupulousness that with us would almost make the stranger think we were observing a religious festival.

Within a hundred miles or so of Yaunde kilometre posts again began to line the road. As I rode along in the moonlight I seemed to pass a great many of them, but it was too dark to read the figures, and I forbore to dismount, hoping that the surprise would be all the greater when dawn came. I got my surprise all right, but it was not the pleasant one I expected and I was shaken to find that I had covered only some twenty miles and that there were another fifty to do. While having a second breakfast I almost decided to take it easy, for I was getting very feeble, the road seemed to be getting worse, and it was doubtful whether I could reach Yaunde that day, much less by midday.

Soon after I had started again, almost reconciled to another night out, the road suddenly began to improve. My flagging energies revived, to receive further stimulus from the sight of the road gang who were responsible for the greatly improved surface. There were several hundred men drawn up in columns of fours, advancing slowly, tamping down the newly laid murram with heavy wooden logs. The logs rose and fell together with a glorious thud which shook the ground, the time being taken from a two-man band which marched in the rear, one man playing a sort of Jew's harp, the other a wooden drum. I could not help reflecting how much better this was in many ways, for the nerves and for employment, than our confounded pneumatic drills.

This excellent hard surface continued all the way. Pedalling like one possessed, I rode a desperate race against time, dismounting at last, limp and wet with sweat, outside the Yaunde post office on the stroke of twelve—to find it did not close until five o'clock.

Waiting for me was a cable telling me to get in touch with the representatives of an old-established west coast firm of Liverpool. At Yaunde, Kribi, Duala, and on the voyage home, I enjoyed their hospitality and assistance.

Yaunde is the administrative capital of the French Cameroons, connected by a railway to Duala, the principal town and port 200 miles away. This was formerly the capital, but when the railway was extended inland to Yaunde the French were wise enough to transfer the seat of administration. It is situated on the central plateau in a hilly, well-wooded region, 2300 feet above sea level. Considering it is only four degrees north of the equator, the climate is pleasant, while fever is almost absent. Compared with the coast itself it is a health resort, and it is much frequented by people from Duala on that account. The European population numbers about two hundred and fifty. There are many well-built, red-tiled bungalows for the officials and an imposing residence for the Governor of the Cameroons. It was interesting to see the unpretentious, democratic site chosen for this building, befitting that of the representative of a republic. It was in the town, with its main entrance opposite to a football ground on which the natives of Yaunde played with much noise every evening. Until then Government House had always conjured up for me a vision of a place set at a respectful distance from the town in the dignified seclusion of its grounds of many acres, so surrounded with trees that all one knew it by was the sentry-box at the gate. This idea is seen at its best or worst in Uganda, where Government House and its satellites have a town of their own (where nothing so plebeian as a shop is allowed), twenty-five miles from the real capital.

The railway terminates at Yaunde, which is thus the collecting centre for the native produce of a large area. Palm oil, palm kernels, cocoa, ground nuts, are brought here to be despatched to the coast, either by the State-owned railway to Duala or by road to Kribi, a smaller port a hundred miles south of Duala. This road, in spite of its narrowness, is a thorn in the flesh of the railway by reason of the number of lorries which ply on it in competition. There is no road to Duala, although the Government are constantly being urged to build one, but as they own the railway their reluctance is very natural.

At Yaunde there are some dozen trading-houses, four of them British. They are all engaged in the same line of business, buying native produce for export, and distributing for native consumption cotton goods, hardware, salt, dried stockfish, wine, and tobacco. Cheap red wine is a very popular drink. The same concerns are found at all the principal trading-centres between Yaunde and the coast, while in important places like Yaunde or Duala some of the bigger ones have three or four branch shops in charge of natives, placed at strategic points to tap the native custom.

Wishing to finish the journey to the sea by road, I decided to go first to Kribi before embarking as arranged at Duala. After three days' rest, I began the last stage inauspiciously by losing myself in the not very extensive suburbs of Yaunde. After two months of Hobson's choice in the matter of roads the offer of more than one proved too embarrassing. With a drop of 2300 feet in front of me I anticipated hopefully that I should now *rouler* to the coast as the eccentric *douanier* had promised, but for the first thirty miles at any rate the road was uphill. Later, when it did begin to descend, the surface was so bad, owing to the lorry traffic and the fact that it was the end of the rainy season, that there was very little free-wheeling at all. As one would expect, the population between Yaunde and the coast is denser (or less scanty), the cultivation more extensive, and the natives more prosperous than in the interior. Some lived in houses, as distinct from huts (I saw several of two stories built of timber), all of which had well-made doors and shuttered windows.

I stopped the night at the house of a local chief in which were three well-furnished rooms. The chief made me a present of eggs (good ones), a compliment which I returned with a 'dash' of five francs. His two intelligent-looking sons both spoke good French and were eager to know what East Africa was like.

At Lolondorf next day, about half-way to the coast, the road becomes so narrow and tortuous that traffic is allowed to move only in one direction. In the morning, until midday, it moves up from the coast, and in the afternoon it leaves Lolondorf for Kribi. If a lorry fails to reach Lolondorf before midday or Kribi before midnight it has to stay where it is, under penalties.

Soon after leaving Lolondorf I was caught by a storm and by the midday exodus of lorries for Kribi. I very willingly left the road to them, for there were about a dozen lorries in the convoy, all driven by light-hearted natives. To be passed by them on a narrow road was a shattering experience.

I took shelter in a hut whose owner was a garrulous old negro in the Uncle Tom tradition. He was busy making a fishing-net, and talked away without looking at his work while his fingers 'netted' automatically. It reminded me of the Kikuyu women I had seen walking in the streets of Nairobi with their fingers busy weaving string bags. I saw the same sort of thing in a village near Bangassu, but there they were weaving mats; men, women, and children, all carrying a piece of mat and weaving it, whether lying, sitting, standing, or walking.

Uncle Tom's remark that 'the rain done finish' was right. I pushed on and had a long, pleasant run through the cool of the evening, coming out at last fairly upon the coastal plain— I had left the hills for good. I found shelter for the night in a hut belonging to a highly 'civilised' citizen who told me he had spent several years in New York working in a laundry. He was very reticent and, to my disappointment, I could get nothing out of him, for it would have been curious to know his reasons for returning, and his opinion of life in this west coast village compared with life in New York—as extreme a contrast as could be imagined.

Only fifty miles remained to be done, but as yet there was no hint that I was approaching the sea. Many days back I had pictured to myself some distant, dramatic glimpse of the Atlantic—something like that of the Pacific which rewarded stout Cortez and his men 'silent upon a peak in Darien,' but no such vision was vouchsafed me. The first I saw of the sea was round the corner of a tin shed in Kribi itself.

Kribi is a small town at the mouth of a large but unnavigable river. There is no harbour, so that ships have to lie out a mile and a half to discharge into surf boats. (The surf on this coast is nothing like so heavy as it is further north outside the Bight.) Kribi's palmiest days were before the War, during the rubber boom, when wild rubber from the forests of the southern Cameroons formed the bulk of the Colony's exports.

The bungalow at which I stopped shared with the lighthouse a small spit of land almost surrounded by river and sea, so that it received what little cool air there was stirring, but, in spite of that, it was sizzling hot.

I came out on the coast on the other side of Africa fifty-six days after leaving Kampala. November 10th was the actual day of my arrival, so that I was just in time to see Kribi 'going gay,' Armistice Day being an official holiday in French Colonies. All the European residents, numbering about fifty, were invited to a dance, while for the natives a programme of sports was arranged, where the great event was a race for war canoes from the bar to the river-mouth. The crews of the six canoes taking part were drawn from different tribes, and the bitterness of their rivalry was excelled only by that of their respective supporters.

Although the crowd lining the shore seemed to find it exciting enough, the race itself was in the nature of a procession, but the real fun started when the winners paddled round the inner harbour, showing off and chanting songs of victory. This ill-timed jubilation was altogether too much for two of the losing crews, who promptly fell upon them, and a fierce naval battle began. Hardwood paddles were broken on harder heads, the crowd on land threw stones and bottles at each with rare impartiality, and finally the canoes capsized, the late occupants swimming ashore to continue the fight on land. Things were really warming up when the native police intervened, chasing away the more active participants and leaving only the greybeards of the rival clans to continue the warfare with vituperation that would have made a fish-wife envious. I was told that this little fracas was the usual custom after the annual canoe race (a more virile form of Boat Race night activities), and it seemed to me a peculiarly appropriate one for Armistice Day.

Harmony was restored in the afternoon when the whole of native Kribi, dressed in European finery, paraded the streets to the music of the town band. These brass bands, peculiar to the Cameroons towns, are a relic of the German days. At Yaunde there was a very grand one dressed in uniform, but it confined itself entirely to pre-War airs—not for sentimental reasons, but because there had been no one to teach them any others.

Canoe race: Canoes going to the starting-point

Same canoe race: The fight at the finish

Two days were spent at Kribi, mostly in the sea, before I mounted the bicycle once again to ride north to Edea, eighty miles away. In that little market town on the Yaunde-Duala line the bell was rung for the last time in Africa and our Odyssey came to an end. From there to Duala there was no way but by rail. I slept by the road for the last time, ten miles short of Edea, riding in at six in the morning to find my prospective host already in the thick of produce buying. At that time of year the produce offering seemed to be mostly cocoa, which was, I imagine, less nauseating to handle at that hour of the morning than palm oil. It was an animated scene, as all the rival stores on opposite sides of the street were hard at it, while the street itself was thronged with natives bringing in produce. The cocoa-beans were brought in baskets as head loads. The load was weighed and examined for dryness, the owner being then offered a price which he either accepted at once or tried to better at one of the rival stores. It was not a pleasant job for the buyers, whose tempers at times must have been sorely tried. The patience shown and the long hours worked by these west coast traders, in a climate inimical to patience or work, impressed me profoundly.

Edea stands on a big river, the Sanaga. Just above the town are the falls, which I saw at their best—a full river pouring a vast volume of water over a straight drop of 130 feet. A few hundred yards below the falls the river flows round an island in two channels, spanned by two mighty bridges, carrying the railway. These were built before the War, and the story goes that the German engineer who built them was later told off to destroy them to delay the British advance when we invaded the Cameroons in 1915. To the astonishment of all, the bridges were found intact, for the father could not bring himself to compass the destruction of his own children.

The bicycle and I brought our labours to an end by taking the train to Duala, a journey of about three hours. Duala is not on the sea, but is situated twenty-three miles up the wide estuary of the Wuri River; opposite, on the north side of the estuary, lie the British Cameroons and the great mass of the Cameroon mountain, an extinct volcano, towering to 13,000 feet. From the upper part of the town one can see in clear weather both the Great and Small Cameroon mountains, and the 9000 feet peak on the island of Fernando Po.

There are about a thousand Europeans and two thousand five hundred natives in the town, which is divided roughly into three parts. The European part, known as Bell, where Germans have been responsible for the general lay-out, boasted many fine avenues and buildings. Evidences of similar careful planning and readiness to spend money can be seen in the ex-German port of Dar-es-Salaam, on the east coast. Lagos, the principal British port on the coast, seems to have grown up fortuitously, for it is a hotch-potch mixture compared with the orderliness of Duala.

I had a few days to wait for a ship, but the time passed pleasantly enough exploring the town and sleeping off the somnolence induced by the west coast delicacies of palm-oil chop and ground-nut stew. Very excellent dishes they are, too, but in my opinion more suitable for the Arctic than the tropics. As their eating necessitates the revivifying effects of much gin, meals in which they figure are serious affairs. On the coast, the day set aside by custom for their consumption is Sunday, just as at home we in England on the same day celebrate the solemn rites of roast beef and Yorkshire pudding.

While waiting for a ship I had leisure to think over the journey which was now ended—a not very eventful journey of 3000 miles across Africa. Satisfaction at getting across was tinged with disappointment at the extraordinary sameness (I had almost said 'tameness') of the scenery of the western half of the journey as compared with the variety seen in the eastern; once the central highlands have been crossed and left behind, the monotony of forest and long grass is all-embracing. Neither is there the great diversity of peoples one meets with in East Africa, where the tribes, differing widely in dress, features, customs, and modes of life, combine with the ever-changing scene to make travel in Kenya, Uganda, or Tanganyika a constant delight. But in spite of the complaint of monotony, which might also be levelled at travel in the desert or the Arctic, for that man who travels by his own exertions no day can be dull and no journey without an abiding interest.

A surprise, perhaps another disappointment, was the comparative ease with which the journey had been done. From what has been said, it should be clear that the sole requisite for success was ability to follow the advice of James Pigg to 'keep tambourine a-roulin.' This absence of

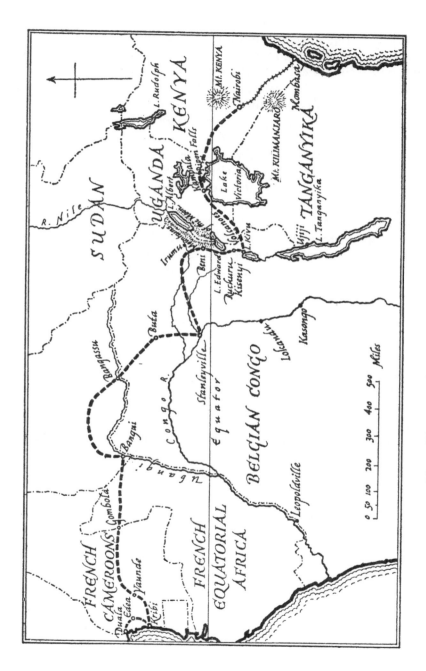

Map 4: The route taken across Africa from east to west

difficulty and danger may be disappointing to others, too, for the tradition of Darkest Africa dies hard. Ten or fifteen years earlier such a ride
would have been difficult enough, if not impossible, and even today
the road is but a slender thread, and Africa, a vast country in which,
away from the road, one can still find the Africa of boyhood's dreams—
the dreams inspired by Rider Haggard, Selous, Stanley. Mechanical
transport has a great deal for which to answer, but even if we use it
there is no reason why we should not deplore it. Modern methods of
transport (perhaps I might be allowed to exclude the push-bike) have
abolished the hardships of African travel, and with them most of the
joys, too—the joys of the march, the camp, the cheery porters. Very
wisely was it said, 'All travel is dull exactly in proportion to its rapidity.'

My ship came up the river and I prepared to embark by buying
myself a coat and a pair of trousers. I was glad that ships tie up alongside a quay at Duala, thus allowing my faithful 'grid' to be wheeled on
board instead of suffering the indignity of being hoisted through the
air like so much inanimate freight. Sailing-day arrived, bringing with
it for me the mingled feelings of most 'last days.' Countries, if lived
and worked in long enough, have a queer way of making a man feel an
affection for them, whether they have treated him well or ill. For fourteen years—a fifth of our allotted span—Africa had been my task-mis-
tress, and now I was leaving her. If she had not given me the fortune I
expected, she had given me something better—memories, mountains,
friends.

We dropped down the river whose muddy waters were soon to be
lost in the clean blue immensity of the sea, while the Cameroon mountain, showing faintly astern, waved to me Africa's last farewell.

H. W. TILMAN

The Collected Edition

FOR THE FIRST TIME SINCE THEIR ORIGINAL APPEARANCE, all fifteen books by H. W. Tilman are being published as single volumes, with all their original photographs, maps and charts. Forewords and afterwords by those who knew him, or who can bring their own experience and knowledge to bear, complement his own understated writing to give us a fuller picture of the man and his achievements. A sixteenth volume is the 1980 biography by J. R. L. Anderson, *High Mountains and Cold Seas*. The books will appear in pairs, one each from his climbing and sailing eras, in order of original publication, at quarterly intervals from September 2015:

www.tilmanbooks.com